POWER FORWARD

My Presidential Education

REGGIE LOVE

Simon & Schuster Paperbacks

New York   London   Toronto   Sydney   New Delhi

Simon & Schuster Paperbacks
An Imprint of Simon & Schuster, Inc.
1230 Avenue of the Americas
New York, NY 10020

One name in this book, "Cal," is a pseudonym.

First Simon & Schuster trade paperback edition January 2016

SIMON & SCHUSTER PAPERBACKS and colophon are registered trademarks of
Simon & Schuster, Inc.

For information about special discounts for bulk purchases,
please contact Simon & Schuster Special Sales at 1-866-506-1949
or business@simonandschuster.com.

The Simon & Schuster Speakers Bureau can bring authors to your live event. For
more information or to book an event contact the Simon & Schuster Speakers
Bureau at 1-866-248-3049 or visit our website at www.simonspeakers.com.

Interior design by Lewelin Polanco

Manufactured in the United States of America

10 9 8 7 6 5 4 3 2 1

The Library of Congress has catalogued the hardcover edition as follows:
Love, Reggie, 1981-
Power forward : my presidential education / Reggie Love.
pages cm
1. Love, Reggie, 1981- 2. Presidents—United States—Staff—Biography.
3. Obama, Barack—Friends and associates. 4. United States—Politics and
government—2001-2009. 5. United States—Politics and government—2009-
I. Title.
E901.1.L68A3 2015
320.092—dc23
[B]
2014040838

ISBN 978-1-4767-6334-7
ISBN 978-1-4767-6335-4 (pbk)
ISBN 978-1-4767-6336-1 (ebook)

CONTENTS

CONTENTS

CONTENTS

I

THE TIP-OFF

The day I met the future president I was wearing the first suit my father ever gave me. A gray Hugo Boss at least a size too big, sloppy and un-tailored. I paired it with a nondescript beige tie and brown Kenneth Cole squared-toe lace-up shoes. I was twenty-three years old, fresh out of Duke University. I thought I looked sharp.

It was December 2005. I had been home killing time for a month in Fayetteville, North Carolina, where my parents lived. I was play-ing round after round of golf while waiting to see if I was going to have a professional sports career (either in NFL Europe or Arena Football, where I could get more experience before hopefully joining the Dallas Cowboys). I was also considering applying for a position at Goldman Sachs. Mostly, I was honing my short game.

My mother, Lynette Love, no fan of idleness, told me I needed a

1

contingency plan beyond pro sports and high finance. "Do something more productive with your time," she scolded as I loafed around her house.

"I've dropped ten strokes off my game!" I shot back, teasing. "I don't know how to be more productive than that."

My mom didn't laugh. And her point was well taken. I wasn't Tiger Woods. Or a retiree. Duly chastened, I sent my résumé to a friend, Alan Hogan, a mentor of a basketball teammate, Andre Buchner, who was close with Sean Richardson, chief of staff to Representative Patrick Kennedy, explaining I might be looking for an internship on Capitol Hill. Not long after, I received a call from Pete Rouse, then chief of staff for Senator Barack Obama. Rouse, I would come to appreciate, was a man of vast experience and abundant talent. He had been chief of staff to Senator Tom Daschle when Daschle was majority leader; around D.C., Pete was known as the 101st senator. My résumé had been forwarded to him because I was young, into sports, African-American, and I'd graduated with a political science degree from Duke.

I knew about Senator Obama. He was the only African-American in the U.S. Senate at the time, and it boggled my mind that 1 percent of the United States Senate was representing 13 percent of America's population. I'd seen his rousing speech at the Democratic National Convention in 2004. And I'd read his book *Dreams from My Father*, in which he plumbed the personal psychology of race in a way I'd not seen discussed before. The parts of the book that addressed Obama's experiences as a black student at an overwhelmingly white, privileged private high school felt as if they had been written just for me.

My family was solidly middle class. Both of my parents went to college at North Carolina Central University, where they met, and at their encouragement I'd attended a private high school that was predominantly well off and Caucasian. So my basketball teammates in the Amateur Athletic League (AAU) constantly gave me grief as the guy who spent more time with whites than blacks on and off the court.

All of my African-American friends who went to public schools saw me as soft. Uncool. Rather than the Fresh Prince, I was the Carlton. And while my prep school friends lived in giant houses and drove luxury cars, my family could barely afford tuition—we were on tuition assistance, and even that was a struggle—and we lived on the other side of town. I felt caught between two worlds: I came from one side, and I wasn't genuinely invited into the other. I was part of both worlds, but didn't fit either mold. After reading *Dreams*, I realized I wasn't the only person of color who felt that way, who'd been struggling with identity, unsure of where he fit.

On the phone, I told Rouse that Senator Obama's book had spoken to me.

"What do you want to do?" he asked.

"I'll do anything," I replied.

He invited me to D.C.

★ ★ ★

I'd been to Washington in May 2001, after Duke won the NCAA Championship. We'd been covered in the media extensively, as every NCAA Championship basketball team has been before and since. Back on campus we were minor celebrities, and now we were in the nation's capital to, among other things, meet the President. Needless to say, it was not your usual introduction to Washington, and my mind was in a thousand places at once.

Our team visited the Pentagon and toured the White House. I remember it was a hot and humid day as we all stood in the Rose Garden sweating in our suits. I was the only one who'd brought a handkerchief, and I passed it around to the guys while we waited for President Bush to show up to welcome us to the White House.

Bush eventually came out, posed, and was very polite. He congratulated us, and that was that. I never thought for a second that

I was standing in the place of my future employment. What I remembered most about D.C., if I'm honest, was a very brief glimpse of the Oval Office, the unpleasant temperature, and how disgusting my handkerchief was after several teammates used it to mop their brows.

When I arrived on a cold winter day in 2005 for the interview with the senator's office, however, it was a different story. I was mesmerized by the federal city. Everything felt so seductively foreign to me. The architecture. The pace. Driving into town felt like being a toddler walking into a toy store. Or buying a new gadget and pushing all the buttons at once. I was overwhelmed, breathless with excitement. Playing hoops for sold-out crowds at Cameron Indoor Stadium or in front of a hundred thousand hand-chopping Florida State University Seminole fans should have prepared me, but the grandness of the city was something completely different.

Which is probably why I crashed the car.

I'd borrowed my father's Volvo S80 to make the drive. I'd never driven in the city before. And though it was a minor fender-bender, a Jeep coming into my lane and hitting the side of my car, I tried not to think of it as a bad omen. (Or of what I was going to tell my dad.)

Senator Obama couldn't meet with me the first day, so I ended up staying overnight with a friend. The next day, I took the Metro over to the Capitol to meet with David Katz, then a personal assistant to the senator. Stepping into the Hart Senate Office Building only reinforced the exhilaration I was already feeling. The place was massive, chock-full of business-attired people rushing past, looking like they were consumed with purpose. There were metal detectors and security guards and men and women in suits and shiny shoes talking in eager, agitated voices into their phones, or to each other. The very air itself seemed heavy with ambition, and as I inhaled it, I realized right then I wanted to be a part of the mix.

I sat outside the cloakroom on a hard wooden bench, too stupid to be nervous, just giddily eager, like a dog in cold weather. The senator emerged with Katz, who pointed at me. I stood up just as he approached.

"Hey, Reggie," Obama said, extending his hand. "Thanks for taking the time."

We shook hello, his demeanor formal, but friendly. He asked what I'd been doing with my life.

"Playing football," I said, adding quickly, "I read your book. It was inspiring, thoughtful."

"That's great. Thank you."

We stood there, eyeing each other. It felt less like a job interview than a sizing up. We both fell silent for a beat, as if we were trying to see who could be more low-key. Then he asked me a couple questions about myself. What mattered to me. What I wanted to do in the future. I didn't have any answers. And I didn't really pretend that I did. I said I was looking forward to learning about the political process, and he said that it was easier to try new things as a young man than when you are thirty-five.

"You think you might want to run for something someday, Reggie?" he asked, finally.

"No. Maybe. If somebody thinks I should." I knew I sounded moronic. I could tell he was unimpressed. He looked me over one last time.

"Well, maybe we'll work something out," he said, then walked away, immediately directing his attention to something that actually mattered.

Nailed it!

Man, did I suck. It was the worst interview I'd ever given. Maybe because it was the *only* interview I'd ever given, aside from trying out for the Duke basketball team, which hardly counted. I left the Hart building that day feeling pretty certain I wouldn't be coming back to D.C. anytime soon.

★ ★ ★

If you had told me then that for the next six years I would spend most of my life crisscrossing the globe with Barack Obama, I would have thought you'd been dropped on your head as a child. And yet that is exactly what happened. He became my boss, and then the President of the United States, and I became what he dubbed his "iReggie," his go-to source for all critical, nonpolitical information.

I was his DJ, his Kindle, his travel agent, his valet, his daughters' basketball coach, his messenger, his punching bag, his alarm clock, his vending machine, his chief of stuff, his note passer, his spades partner, his party planner, his workout partner, his caterer, his small forward, his buffer, his gatekeeper, his surrogate son, and ultimately, improbably, luckily, his friend.

For the entirety of my stint in Washington, I was at the senator-then-president's side for more hours a day than not. From dawn to what was often the middle of the night, I was a witness not only to history, but to a side of the man few got to see: an attentive father, a devoted husband, a trash-talking basketball player, a feisty card shark, a loyal and thoughtful friend with a wicked sense of humor. I also saw him in those early morning hours on the campaign trail when no one believed in him; eating lunch alone in the White House; flipping through a stack of magazines; shooting free throws in deserted small-town high school gymnasiums; taking a few moments to compose himself in the seconds before stepping onstage to be sworn in as the 44th President of the United States of America.

Being a personal assistant, a "bodyman," is like taking a ball from half court and trying to heave it into the basket. You don't know how it is really going to work out. Luckily, we grew close over time, and what originally seemed like a low percentage Hail Mary ended up being a more manageable job than I would have anticipated. Perhaps most surprisingly, we became friends, eventually even something close to family.

I carried snacks and the luggage, babysat for the children of world leaders, prepped the teleprompter and the operator, and handled a million other tasks that came up on the fly. Most of all, I listened. Gradually, I came to understand with one look from the President what sort of day lay ahead.

Because I was not part of the political process, in many ways I became the President's touchstone for normalcy. His window onto the outside world. We played basketball together. (A *lot* of basketball.) We played cards. We debated the merits of Tony Parker and rehashed *Mad Men* plotlines. We watched ESPN. I was twenty-one years younger than him. We didn't have a lot in common in terms of life experience, but what we did share was safe ground. I wasn't going to question him about the economy or deliver bad news about the polls. And because of that, the time we spent together was unique. I was able to see through a rare window that others did not. I would occasionally let fly with an expletive when we talked. So did he. The subject was usually basketball.

★ ★ ★

Five days after my abysmal interview, Pete Rouse called me back. I would soon learn that not many things would get done without him. Rouse was my mentor and champion, as he was for many people on the Hill. He had a vision and game plan for me.

"You have good presence," he said. "We want you to come to D.C. and grow with this team."

I didn't really know what he was talking about. And I told him as much.

"Are you sure?" I asked.

He said he was.

"I'm not certain I want to make a long-term commitment," I said, backpedaling.

7

"That's fine. We can start you at twenty-eight thousand."

Not exactly what my fellow Duke graduates were earning at Goldman Sachs and Morgan Stanley. Not exactly NFL coin either.

"Do I get moving expenses? A signing bonus?"

"No."

I mulled over the offer, remembering the energy I'd felt when I visited Washington, remembering, too, how impressed I'd been with Senator Obama.

"When do I start?" I asked.

"Just get here by January."

★　★　★

I took the position for many reasons, some more thought through than others. I liked the sense of working for a larger purpose I'd observed and felt when I was in D.C. Another thing stuck with me from that visit, too: the lack of racial diversity in America's political system. I also knew that I wanted to work for someone I respected, admired, and could learn from. And Senator Barack Obama was that.

I had little inkling then of just how epic his impact would be, not only on this country, but on me as I grew into an adult. At his side, I would learn the key lessons of what makes a leader, a pioneer, a man. His example (combined with the examples set by my father and my coaches) led me down the path to adulthood. I would come of age in the course of this extraordinary journey.

I knew none of this, of course, when I said yes to the job. But I'd watched and rewatched the senator's convention speech on You-Tube. He reminded me of my pastor. He was a man of mettle and determination. He was going to change the political landscape.

And I was going to be there while he did.

2

THE BOTTOM IS ONLY THE BEGINNING

I was hired as a staff assistant. On January 6, 2006, I moved into a crappy apartment in northeast D.C., on Ninth between F and G. It was a thousand-dollar-a-month dump with mold on the ceilings and rats, in a neighborhood where my car was broken into like it was a paper sack.

During an early meeting in the senator's office, Pete Rouse called all the staff assistants to the table and asked us what we'd like to do. It was an impressive, even intimidating, office. My eyes jumped from Rouse to the eight-by-ten portrait of Justice Thurgood Marshall to my fellow assistants to the senator's autographed gloves from Muhammad Ali. I was inspired just sitting there. As we were rapidly laying claim to various jobs, it became clear that no one wanted to handle mail. Since his DNC speech, the senator had received something like ten thousand pieces of correspondence, backlogged from 2004. The job of sorting and cataloging the input would be a massive, thankless one. Never one to shy away from a challenge, I volunteered.

To me, it was a concrete undertaking. I had always been drawn to measurable outcomes. It was part of why I enjoyed playing sports. At the end of the day, you knew where you stood. You won or lost— simple.

In the mail room, I implemented systems to help improve the office's "constituent services," which were basically methods for tracking the mail and speeding up the time it took to respond. I used Adobe, Excel, an FTP with the sergeant at arms office, and other software to digitize, manage, and track the flood of letters. And from the positive chatter in the senator's office (Pete Rouse was impressed), you'd have thought I'd turned water into wine. In a way I had. I'd accepted the lowliest job and converted it into something that attracted attention. People on staff began to wonder, what else can he do?

To supplement my meager salary, I worked part-time as a bouncer at McFadden's Irish pub. It was your typical preppy D.C. college hangout. One of my oldest friends, Cory Broadnax, was already working there part-time as a bouncer. We had been college teammates at Duke, where he played defensive lineman, and we had known each other since we were fifteen and playing AAU basketball. Now we'd reconnected, and Cory said working at McFadden's was easy money and fun. It mostly was, until the night some drunk frat boy threw a punch at me.

The kid didn't have I.D., so I couldn't let him in. "Come on, bro," he begged, giving me a little smirk.

"Sorry, I don't make the rules," I explained.

"You think you can tell me what to do?" he spat back, his face suddenly flooding red. He was dressed in khakis, a pastel-pink J.Crew button-down. His friends were all staring at him. But he only had eyes for me. "You think you're somebody? You trying to push me around?"

I'll give it to the guy. It took some stones to pick a fight with somebody three times his size. Of course, he was also drunk. Liquid courage, it is well documented, can convince you that a host of bad ideas are, in fact, good ones.

And then he swung.

Thankfully, it was a big windup. I saw his fist coming a mile away and moved out of the way. Cory also noticed what was happening and jumped in, wrapping his arms around the guy's pink shirt, jerking him forcefully from my reach.

"How dare you!" he sputtered as his friends tried to drag him away. "You're just a fucking doorman."

Well, now *I am,* I thought. But a doorman is just a job. Jobs change. Being entitled, with no self-awareness, rarely does.

I stopped working at McFadden's shortly after that. I had recently gotten promoted at the senator's office, and frankly, I was run ragged from being up nearly twenty-two hours every other day. Besides, I couldn't show up at the Obama office with a black eye. That's not the kind of operation they were running.

Thankfully, after six months working for the senator in the mail room, I was promoted from staff assistant to deputy political director for Alyssa Mastromonaco at Obama's Hope Fund. I would be splitting my time between the Senate office and his PAC. Once again, I landed in a very glamorous position: database management.

If Senator Obama did a fundraiser, if he was in a TV advertisement to help another candidate, if he sent out an email asking for a contribution for someone else's campaign, if he appeared at a rally—any communication he had with *anybody*—I kept a record of it.

This kind of list is part of a politician's lifeline. The ability to differentiate an avid supporter from an ambivalent one is of profound value. So when someone requested a photograph with Senator Obama at a Democratic meeting, we'd promise to mail it to that person if he or she would provide an address, and I would make sure that happened and then keep track of that information. The PAC also used postcards to build relationships with the thousands of non-Illinois constituents the senator would meet while campaigning for other Democrats. The team would send a photo of the senator standing in a location that the recipient would immediately recognize as local, and we'd personalize the postcard with a note on the back saying, "Hey, thanks for joining me at the rally in support of Claire McCaskill" or "Debbie Stabenow." And with the note would be a link to our website.

The postcard was good PR. But the genius part was collecting names and email addresses. It would become the beginning of the first national list of supporters. It is always the efforts of a couple hundred dedicated individuals that allow a candidate to build broader support, and even before any official declaration of candidacy, the team had started to identify who those few hundred people were.

In part because of the systems I helped to set up, the campaign was allowed to buy/rent fewer lists in the future, which, in turn, enabled the team to communicate coherent messages and to interact with engaged and likely voters. Identifying and interacting with Democratic activists across the country before officially launching a national campaign was critical. Preparation and forward thinking had the Obama team slightly ahead of the curve. The team could identify among the people we'd mailed, who had already shown up to see the Senator, those who had already demonstrated tangible support. The team was able to put energy into smarter places. The data was solid. Because of that I felt I'd helped to make a difference early on.

Even so, the process wasn't easy. There were days when I would have more than a thousand postcards to send. I'd bring them home with me and stamp them one after another, hour after hour in front of the television. Sometimes I'd enlist friends to help. (Bribing them with beer or chips or the use of my pickup truck to move furniture.)

There was something else the team did differently. In the normal ecosystem of campaigning, interested parties would ask Barack Obama to appear at an event to help with their fundraising. Typically special guests like Obama would do their thing, help draw a crowd to other candidates and causes, then say good luck and God bless. But early on, our approach to events had a longer-term goal in mind.

In our scenario, we adopted the philosophy that "Obama's a Democrat. We are trying to get you reelected because you are a Democrat, and hopefully we can all grow together." And so, when the senator agreed to appear, we made the request that his participation be contingent on our receiving the list for the event of the candidate he was showing up to support.

This did not always go over well.

The Iowa Democratic Party, for example, gave us their list, not digitally, but as labels. The kind your grandmother sticks on envelopes. I had to type thousands of addresses and names into our database. It was a passive-aggressive "screw you." But we got the data.

These were the early days. I only knew the senator well enough to say hello coming and going. I felt like to him I was probably still some random staffer who happened to have played basketball at Duke.

I did get to sit in on one meeting. It was with Baron Davis, the two-time NBA all-star, who came in with his agent, Cash Warren, to talk about his youth development foundation. I was a prop. But it was still cool to have that seat at the table, even if it was only for fifteen minutes. I remember thinking how in awe I was to be in the senator's office with such an impressive bunch. Baron Davis had the basketball career I always wanted and not only was killing it, he was able to work with his best friend, Cash, on the daily. I was impressed, and a bit jealous.

At this point, the senator hadn't yet formally declared an intention to run for the highest office of the land. I was down on the bottom rungs of the office ladder, developing these systems, gathering the data, doing the tedious work, not really having a clear endgame in mind. Little did I know how dramatically everything was about to change. How, in a matter of days, Senator Obama would go from a passing figure to a presidential candidate, and I would play the role of sidekick.

★ ★ ★

It was Pete Rouse's idea. It had probably been his plan all along. He brought me into his office, sat me down, and gave me two scenarios.

"Do you want to go to Iowa?" he asked.

"Do I?" I asked, not knowing what "going to Iowa" meant— other than the fact that if I did go, the population of black people would increase exponentially.

Then he brought up the prospect of my being the senator's personal aide.

"Is that an option?" I asked, knowing even less about what that job would look like.

"It is. But I didn't think you were interested in that position," Rouse said casually.

He wasn't wrong. I was young, ambivalent about almost everything except basketball, but especially about being a personal aide, because I had no notion of what it entailed. On the other hand, there was my desire to shoot hoops. Hang out with my friends. Maybe get a flashy job in finance like some of my old classmates. Or pursue my dream of playing in the NFL one day, something I'd been groomed for since high school and had been actively recruited for after graduating from Duke. Being someone's personal aide sounded like the very opposite of all of that. But Rouse had never led me astray, and his offer resonated with my instinct to get off the bench and into the game in any way I could make a difference.

At the time, I was dating a young woman named Erin, who worked as an analyst for Prudential Securities. I'd met her through her sister, Casey, who was in Duke law school while I was an undergrad. Erin was my ambassador to D.C. She was twenty-nine and dialed into the local ethos. She thought I was too immature for her, and I probably was, but we dated anyway. She ended up being a great advisor to me; an unanticipated inspiration—a friend with *actual* benefits. If I ever got lost driving in D.C., I would call her, and she would navigate me home. At base, she had figured her shit out. And I hadn't.

"Don't be stupid," Erin chided, when I told her I was probably going to pass on the traveling personal assistant offer. "This is the biggest opportunity of your life. My last boyfriend was a field organizer in Iowa for Kerry and if your candidate doesn't win it's tough. But, as a personal assistant to a candidate, win or lose, you are left with invaluable experience and relationships."

Erin was always ten moves ahead of me. She could see the smart play, how the job of PA to Barack Obama would change my life forever, in ways that running a campaign office in Iowa, or working at Goldman Sachs, or training for the Dallas Cowboys would not.

It was Erin's voice I heard in my head when I walked into Rouse's office and told him I wanted the bodyman slot after all. And just like that, I had a new job.

What I didn't have was a job description. To this day I still haven't been able to track it down, because there never was one. Each bodyman job is unique to the principal. Every boss is peculiar. Like snowflakes, the bosses come with their own distinct characteristics (and needs). And more likely than not, they don't even know what those needs are—until you don't meet them.

On that note, to any future PA candidates out there, know this: nobody is going to tell you what you are supposed to do. There is no training. There is no manual. There is no human resource department to provide you with a helpful itemized sheet of responsibilities. If you dare to ask what your job actually is, the folks in charge will likely say, "Handle stuff."

That's it. "Handle stuff."

Thus was the true beginning of my presidential education. Learning the ropes of life at the heel of the man who was out to change the course of this great nation.

As for how you "handle stuff"? You're on your own. You will be clueless. You will panic. On more than one occasion, said "stuff" will most definitely *not* be handled. You will mess it up. Royally.

I know I did.

3

EVERY LAYUP ISN'T EASY

On February 1, 2007, the night before my first official trip as bodyman, I was walking the aisles of pharmacy-turned-supermarket Harris Tee- ter in something of a fog. I had black and silver Sharpies in my basket, black Pilot G2 Gel Roller pens, Trident chewing gum. I was think- ing I should throw in some trail mix, in case the guy was starving or something.

So I headed to the nut section and confronted how much I did *not* know about Senator Obama. Considering all the options—salted or dry roasted? sweet or spicy? with or without dried fruit or candy?— I realized I hadn't a clue what the man would like. I also had an ac- companying thought: how much could it possibly matter? The con- tingency I was planning for was a starving candidate. He'd be grateful regardless, right?

I snagged a bag of Planters Trail Mix Fruit & Nut with M&M's.

Back in my apartment, I couldn't relax. I was anxious. I tried to watch some TV to distract myself, and before I knew it, I woke up at 1:00 A.M. and realized I'd been drooling all across my shoulder. I walked to the bedroom to try to catch some real sleep, all too aware that in four and a half hours I would be boarding a commercial flight from D.C. to LaGuardia with the senator. He had just formed an exploratory committee to test his viability for becoming the President of the United States. And we were heading to New York City for three fundraisers—cocktails, a dinner, and a late-night meet and greet.

I'd already gotten my feet wet doing some advance work in Washington. I'd been the point of contact for the "Families USA" conference, where the senator delivered one of his first speeches on health care in the U.S., articulating his belief that our country needed to create a supplementary system for the traditional employer-based insurance system, which he hoped would act as a transition to universal health coverage.

As part of the advance team, I'd arrived at the venue, the Mayflower Hotel, early enough to absorb the layout, confirming that the entrance and exit routes wouldn't be too congested for the senator to travel through. The narrower a route, the more time it took for him to leave a building. In my short time as a newly minted PA, I'd observed that Senator Obama was a man of the people and he never turned his back on an opportunity to hear another point of view. Which could make for a prolonged exit.

The day prior to our trip to New York, I worked advance for the National Prayer Breakfast at the Washington Hilton. My responsibility was to make sure that the Senator got from the breakfast to the car in a timely manner, so that he wasn't late to his next scheduled event. It seemed simple enough. The prayer breakfast officially ended at 9 A.M., so at about eight-fifty, I walked toward the entrance of the ballroom in anticipation of the senator's exit. It was then that I noticed he was not at his table. After a thorough search around the room, I realized that he wasn't there at all.

I tried my best to stay composed. It was my trial run before my first travel assignment with the candidate, and I'd already misplaced him. *Aha! I know. I'll just call him on his cell phone.*

I rang the number I had in my cell and got a voicemail saying that his number had been changed. Panic began to set in. I'd lost Barack Obama. I called Nick Colvin, another team member.

"Nick," I said, trying to feign calm, "what's the senator's cell phone number? I can't seem to locate him."

"He's been in the car for ten minutes," Nick replied.

"Oh, okay, cool," I stammered, though cool was the last thing I felt. Especially since I was about to formally begin my tenure as the bodyman in less than twenty-four hours.

Turns out, I had been right to be anxious. Losing the soon-to-be presidential candidate was the opening chapter in a long catalog of errors I would commit over the next six years. Another memorable, if insignificant, error occurred on the flight into LaGuardia, when the senator opened the bag of trail mix I'd bought and proceeded to pick out every M&M, holding them all in his palm like pieces of candy-coated toxic waste.

"I'm not going to eat these," he said, pushing his hand in my general direction. *Clearly,* I thought. "Do you want them?" he asked, wrinkling his nose.

"No thank you, sir," I answered, then made the first of what would be thousands of notes to self: No candy with the trail mix.

This list would also come to include:

No gum wrapped in tiny papers. (He preferred Dentyne Ice.)
No energy bars with fruit. (Likewise, he preferred MET-Rx
   Protein Plus.)
Salads only in emergencies, because you can't eat salad in a car.

Nothing battered and fried.

Always have extra hand sanitizer, because after a day spent on
a rope line you go through that stuff like oxygen.

Don't forget the silverware.

Or the napkins.

Or the water.

Or the green tea.

Nicorette. Normal flavor, two milligrams. (Like Sharpies and
regular gum, I would buy that stuff by the case.)

And heading the list: Little things matter. Subhead:

Sometimes they make all the difference.

★ ★ ★

Traveling to New York always feels magical to me—ever since my
first trip to the Big Apple in December 2001, when Duke played
Kentucky in Madison Square Garden and Coach K led our team to
Ground Zero. On this inaugural trip to New York for the campaign
the city still had a sense of grandeur to me. We would be attending
a couple of fundraisers and then an event hosted by Tracy Maitland,
one of the most powerful African-American men in media, someone
I had long admired and respected.

Maitland had put together a who's who of African-American
moguls, including Russell Simmons, Pepsi guru Frank Cooper, fi-
nancier Brian Mathis, L.A. Reid, Andre Harrell, and about fifteen
others who were set to meet Obama in Maitland's swanky West Vil-
lage apartment.

I was inspired just breathing in the same oxygen. I mean, these
were men of color who had broken barriers in corporate America
and crushed it in everything they'd tried in life. I was still very much
a small-town boy from North Carolina. The only super-successful
black men I'd known until then were in the sports world. Meeting

these kingmakers and seeing all these alternate paths to achievement gave me a perspective that I'd never had before.

Despite the fact that most of these men had overcome racial challenges in their own careers, many of them were not as eager to jump on the Obama bandwagon as I thought they would have been, especially given that executives and boards of directors at Fortune 500 companies were even less diverse than the executive, legislative, and judicial branches of government. To say this group was rough on Obama is like saying the Pistons were rough on Jordan. Forget the Jordan rules. These were the Obama rules. It seemed like I was watching a trial. The candidate was seated in the front of the room, and everyone else was lined up across from him, grilling him like a steak.

Why was he the man for the job? They didn't see what Obama had done *specifically* for the black community. African-Americans had loved Bill Clinton, who over the years had forged relationships of reciprocal trust with concrete action, and this group of heavy hitters wasn't certain Obama would have their back the way that Clinton had. There was a lot of hand-wringing over the fact that the senator hadn't spent enough time in the African-American churches, or courting nationally prominent African-American politicians and leaders and their organizations.

Over the next couple of hours, the candidate gave the men detailed descriptions of all the things he had worked on up to that point and explained why he might be unfamiliar to them. "I've only been a United States senator for two years," he offered. And he spelled out in detail how he had spent his time among his constituents—the African-American community on Chicago's South Side. He'd also helped the Democrats win back the Senate in 2006, a feat that promised tangible benefits for millions of Americans, African-Americans included.

The back-and-forth struck me as bizarre. Like a great many Americans, I had reasonably assumed that the elite African-American bloc would automatically be on the senator's team. But, like everyone else he would come to meet during the campaign, they wanted to know who was going to carry their water. The men in that meeting—they just didn't know Barack Obama. They weren't yet aware of his depth, his core values. In a nutshell, they made the case that while the candidate might be black, he might not be *black enough*.

As I watched the scene unfold, it was hard to keep my jaw from falling open. I was like, *The guy's running for president and he's qualified, he has a chance, and he looks like you! This is amazing!* In my mind there was no scenario where another African-American would have doubted for a second that Obama was the right person for the position. Not black *enough*? How was that even possible?

The event was scheduled to last forty-five minutes. It ended up lasting two and a half hours. The entire meeting was uncomfortable for me because (1) of all people, I thought these guys would be easy, or at least relatively easy, and (2) there I was, some wild-eyed kid in charge of moving Senator Barack Obama along to the hotel before 12 A.M. so that he could get some semblance of a night's sleep before continuing on the campaign trail the next day, and I had no clue how to pull him out or if I even should. (I didn't.)

That was the day I learned that in politics, as in life, there are no easy plays. If you want someone in your corner, you have to earn his or her support.

Even when you think you have all the right factors in your favor, in other words, you still manage to find out that not all layups are easy.

The senator closed the meeting by saying, "If I'm out there running for president as Barack Hussein Obama, African-American, regardless of whether I win or lose, that in itself does more for your cause than anything we've spoken about today. It takes the roof off the glass ceiling for all our children. There ends up being nothing our children feel they can't do."

Everyone in that room would ultimately throw his support behind the senator's campaign, but it took some time to win the love.

That night when I went back to the W Hotel at 49th and Lexington, a place that would became very familiar over the campaign, I finally exhaled. I wanted to process what had just happened, but there was no time. So it would be for the next several years. I knew I felt a peculiar sense of purpose and destiny, but I also had to curate and respond to hundreds of emails and print out the briefings for the next day. The Barack Obama for President train had officially left the station. And it was now my job to help it run on time.

4

YOU CAN'T TEACH HEIGHT

I was a lucky kid. For starters, my parents, Lynette and Richard Maurice Love Sr., stayed married. That was not the case for many of my friends. I was raised Southern Baptist at Friendship Missionary Baptist Church on Beatties Ford Road in Charlotte, where Pastor Jones not only preached the gospel but showed me the value of the strength of community. My parents put a premium on keeping promises, particularly ones made in front of God.

I can see, looking back, how the solidarity between my mother and father, their example of sticking it out through the tough times, equipped me for success, and especially for taking risks. I grew up knowing two things for certain. First, my parents loved me. Second, their unconditional love was not the same as having their respect. That needed to be earned, not taken for granted.

When I was about six and still had training wheels on my bicycle, I decided to take them off myself. My older brother had a two-wheel bike, so I wanted one as well. I used my father's wrench to detach the training wheels, then taught myself how to ride without them (though for the first month, I could only ride in a counterclockwise circle). When they came home from work, I proudly showed my dis-believing parents what I had done.

Even then, I liked challenges. That remains true today. Every time I meet one goal, I crave another. I am one of those people who always want to figure out the limitations of any situation. What can I do? What can I get away with doing? When I was a kid, if no one bothered to tell me the rules, I would push the boundaries until I found the line. Often, I crossed it.

In Newell Elementary School, where I struggled with sitting still and staying focused, I found what I thought was an opportunity to sell cigarettes to my classmates. My mother brought them home from her job at the Philip Morris tobacco company. No one in our immedi-ate family was a regular smoker, so cartons of perfectly good cigarettes were languishing in the garage and her car. In the early nineties there was no shortage of kids in the fourth and fifth grades who believed smoking was cool. It didn't take long for me to do the math.

When I finally got caught—well, ratted out by a classmate who had been busted by his parents—my mom sat me down and lectured me about the evils of tobacco. I explained to her that I didn't smoke, then politely asked why I should be punished because other people did.

My logic went over with Mom about as well as you might ex-pect, but I wasn't being clever. At school, I'd seen an entrepreneurial opportunity. A window to step through. And that excited me. It still does.

I believe in the saying that success is where preparation meets opportunity. You never know when or where the opportunity will come—but when you do get the chance and your number is called, you want to be able to look yourself in the mirror and say, "Hey, I was prepared, I gave it everything I had and put in the work." (Even if that work is peddling smokes on the playground.)

That said, no matter how much preparation I did, I was never a great student. I got average grades. My parents felt that a more demanding environment might inspire me, so after middle school, they enrolled me in Providence Day, a private prep school on the other side of town, in southeast Charlotte. Tuition was about $12,000 a year. More than we could afford. But my folks were determined to give me the best opportunities they could.

Because my grades weren't the best, I had to sign up for remedial math courses over the summer just to get caught up for my first day of ninth grade. I hated it. All I wanted to do was play basketball. I may have been an outcast on my block and in my new largely white classroom, but sports, at least, was a reliable equalizer in both neighborhoods. Every hour spent working at math was an hour not spent working on my game. My parents, my mother especially, made sure I stayed focused on the long game of academics.

When I was in seventh grade and still in public school, basketball and popularity were for me synonymous. I'd been cut from my junior high team. Two seventh graders made the squad, and I wasn't one of them. My only option was to play in the recreational league during the winter season, while all my friends got to represent their school teams. I complained and cried to my father that it wasn't fair. He listened for a while, but then, fed up with my self-pity, he flatly stated the truth: "You're not that good." And then he asked the only relevant question, "Do you want to play basketball or not?"

I insisted I did, and he said, "Then play your best on the team that you can play on."

I didn't know it then, but that recommendation would carry me through decades of decision making. If anything, having something to prove made me work harder.

I made the school team the following season, my eighth grade year. I kept excelling, eventually becoming the leading scorer. By the end of high school I was named Male Athlete of the Year by *The Charlotte Observer*. It was such a gratifying feeling to start at the bottom and pull myself up rung by rung.

My father used to tell me all the time, "Reggie, you gotta do the work. Sports or school, it doesn't matter. The work won't do itself, and if you choose not to do the work, then you should never be surprised about the outcome, because you chose to leave it up to chance."

All of that was true, of course. But there was something else he told me that struck an even deeper chord.

After getting cut in seventh grade, I practiced more than any other kid in my neighborhood. My friends made fun of me for having to play on a rec league team, which only made me want to play and practice all the more. I improved, I grew, getting both taller and stronger. But not enough. When my AAU squad didn't qualify for a national tournament, the teams that did qualify picked up players from teams that hadn't, to fill out their roster. Being my team's leading rebounder and scorer, I was confident my name would be called. But it wasn't. I was passed over for a thirteen-year-old kid who was six-foot-five.

I was stunned.

"But I was the best player," I said to my father.

He listened and nodded slowly. "Reggie, you know it's tough. I think you are better than the other kid, but you can't teach height."

I didn't get it at the time, but eventually, I saw that my dad was imparting to me that life isn't fair, and even when you perform at your peak, it may not be enough to overcome the circumstances on any given day.

I have since seen my father's adage play out in many arenas. You can substitute "height" for "race," "gender," "income," "geography," "legacy," "class." Just because you work harder doesn't mean everything is going to go according to plan.

★ ★ ★

That you can't teach height certainly became clear in the early stages of the campaign when the Obama team couldn't get unbiased media coverage. After the senator announced, he did the living room tour. We traveled the country, and he sat in people's homes and listened to them describe what they wanted from their government and from a leader. It was glaringly obvious that Americans were hungry for something different. They wanted fresh ideas. Passion. In every town, people would come at him with a barrage of questions and needs. Obama was consistently surprised at the intensity. Everywhere, people wanted the same thing: something new.

Even so, the powers that be would not support the candidate because it was too early, or he was too green, or they were already backing Hillary Clinton. We got beat up in the press on similar grounds. Dismissed. Never more so than in 2007, after the *New York Times* ran a column suggesting that Clinton was going to be the party nominee, and Obama should face the inevitable, pack his bags, and go home to Chicago.

We'd spent the night before in West Palm Beach, Florida. An old friend I knew from Duke was in Miami, and she'd come to visit me. She ended up staying the night.

The next morning, the senator let himself into my room using the Secret Service keys that accessed every room, including, when need be, his. I was up and getting all my things together, but my friend was still in bed. I remember the most peremptory of knocks, the sound of his voice talking even as he walked in. The stresses of the campaign, the piece in the *Times*—he was charged up, going a mile a minute.

"Hey, Reggie, we need to go over the schedule"—at which point the senator finally noticed my friend in bed, covers pulled to her throat, mortified.

"Oh," he said. "I apologize." Then he turned around and hurried out.

"Was that?" she asked, face red.

"Senator Barack Obama," I said sheepishly.

Later, the team was piled into a small plane, another day of grueling campaigning ahead of us, when the candidate turned to his senior advisor David Axelrod and began venting to him about getting his ass kicked in the media and how exhausting the entire process was in every imaginable way and all for so little reward. Everyone was quiet, so I chimed in from the seat behind him, "You know, sir, if it's any consolation, I'm having the time of my life."

And the senator said to me, "Well, Reggie, it's actually *not* a consolation to me that my campaign for president can help subsidize your love life."

There was weak laughter from Axelrod, Robert Gibbs (our communications director and future White House press secretary), and Marvin Nicholson, but none from Obama.

For the candidate, the death march of the campaign was punishing. He was away from his wife and daughters. He was risking everything and getting zero payoff. Instead, he was being written about as a neophyte on a fool's errand. I tried again.

"Actually, sir, I got way more action in college."

A round of groans rose up from the whole staff. If nothing else, I was providing a distraction from the gloom. I'd uncovered another facet to the bodyman role: that of court jester.

Reading the news coverage, the evidence was clear. My father had been right. You can't teach height. We couldn't sway the national press to our belief that we had more to offer than an eminent political family. That our Bad News Bears, ragtag team would in fact turn out to be the best option for a new America. So, after those initial defeatist days, we stopped paying attention to the pundits who counted us out.

We quit reading the negative coverage. It was what I learned playing sports: You don't listen to the chatter about your team or your game. The guy who can't play at all and probably never played always has the most to say about the guy who is actually on the court. You stay informed, but you don't let the criticism sink in or sink the team. Never believe how bad or how great people say you are. My coach would say that when you go back to watch the tape of a game, you see that you were never as great as you remember or as bad as you remember.

When our efforts were questioned, the candidate would say, "Come see us in Iowa."

And what do you know? They did. They really, really did.

5

NEVER GET TOO COMFORTABLE ON THE BENCH

I enrolled at Duke in the summer of 2000 with a full football scholarship as a wide receiver. My mother was never a fan of the game of football, believing that it was too violent. She always stressed the importance of education, and I was sure to get that at Duke. And after four years at Providence Day, surrounded by wealth and the evidence of the opportunities that it affords, I was also ready to leverage my athleticism. Football was my ticket. I was in great shape. I knew the Blue Devils playbook. Sure, I was eager to embrace the freedom of living in a new town, away from family. Mostly, however, I was ready to play football.

I was recruited by Clemson, Florida State, USC, Florida, and Tennessee, but I chose Duke for their academics (I knew how injuries happened) and because their basketball program was decent.

I knew they didn't think I was good enough for the hoops team, but in the back of my mind I thought, maybe if I was on campus, I could make a miracle happen.

I showed up freshman year primed and pumped, eager to compete, with an ego the size of Texas. But I hardly played at all in the first eight games. My *roommate* played, which stung, but not as much as the fact that the football team I'd selected to pin my future on didn't win a single game all season. It was, in a word, a letdown.

Five weeks into the season, I still wasn't getting any snaps, but the schoolwork had filled the void by kicking my butt. I was surprised by how demanding the classes were. So there I was, struggling on two counts, not exactly the BMOC I'd imagined I would be. I found myself sliding into what I look back on as a mild depression.

Up until then, I'd derived all my value from winning. Now I wasn't just losing; I wasn't even qualified to play with a team that couldn't win a game. I was down because, well, as much as it pained me to admit it, I'd thought I was better than I was.

The struggle would turn out to be great preparation for the exploratory primary days of the campaign with Senator Obama, when we all had such high hopes and boundless conviction and were treated as if we were party crashers, literally. There was a gulf between how we perceived ourselves, and our chances, and what the outside world felt. Those were the days when every newspaper headline was telling the Obama camp to concede defeat, that the team lacked the track record to succeed, that we were a drain on political resources, and that the whole Democratic Party would thrive if all the candidates would just step aside and usher the next Clinton president all the way to 1600 Pennsylvania Avenue.

When I played football at Duke, the vibe was similar, but of much less national importance. We didn't win a game for two seasons. But we still had to show up as if the last loss hadn't happened. We had to refuel and believe. We prepared with the faith that every game we played in we had a chance to win. It was the same story on the campaign. No one outside the team thought we were going to win. We were good—just not good enough in the eyes of mainstream media.

It was not until the second to last game, Duke at Georgia Tech, that I saw real playing time. We still hadn't nabbed a win, and starter Jeremy Battier (my roommate) was about to go in, when he couldn't find his mouthpiece. Bam, just like that, I was finally up.

We ended up losing that game as well. But I caught my first career touchdown pass, one of only a few for our team that season. It was a small beacon of light that showed me that maybe I wasn't as bad as I was starting to believe. Maybe there was hope for me yet.

★ ★ ★

The silver lining throughout that tough freshman year was hoops. Basketball has been a constant in my life. Whenever times feel daunting—in college, on the campaign, during my stint in the White House, even now—I know I can always turn to the basketball court to set my head straight.

Some nights after a long practice, I'd let myself into the Brodie Gymnasium near my dorm on Duke's east campus and shoot alone for hours. It was my meditation. My church. My home away from home.

I would play hoops until 11 P.M., midnight, later. The football coaching staff knew I was there, and I think at times they questioned my commitment to Duke football. I understood their concerns, but it wasn't about my commitment to football; it was more about my passion for basketball.

From the moment I started playing, I've always loved the game. Like most kids, football and basketball filled up many of my hours, and I was fiercely competitive at both, but basketball was my favorite.

If it was snowing or raining outside, I would back my parents' cars out of the garage so I could practice my dribbling on the cement floor. My football coaches were always urging me to bulk up, so I did hundreds of crunches, hundreds of push-ups. But no matter how tired strength training left me at the end of the day, I always wanted to hoop.

On paper it made no sense for me to spend all my extra time on the court. I didn't fool myself. Basketball wasn't going to get me a scholarship at a college that met my interests in education, nor was the NBA ever going to be my career. I was, ironically, much better at football than basketball. But the minute football season ended, I ate, slept, and lived basketball. My football coaches didn't love that habit either. They wanted to know why I wasn't resting or watching film.

In a way, I was training for the job I wanted, not the job I had. I may have been better suited to one sport. But my passion was with another.

It was a dilemma I would go on to encounter in various permutations throughout the next decade. Do you stick with the position you've mastered? Or do you push yourself to master the position that seems out of reach? Do you listen to what everyone else thinks is best for you? Or do you listen to your own voice? Do you settle? Or do you dream?

I chose to dream.

★ ★ ★

The summer before my senior year of high school, I'd submitted my highlight tape, which David Carrier (my high school coach) had put together for me, to a couple of the Duke basketball coaches. I also had the amazing good fortune to play in front of Mike Krzyzewski, "Coach K," whose daughter, Jamie Krzyzewski, played girls' basketball for a rival high school (Durham Academy). I scored 32 points and snagged twenty rebounds—a performance that I prayed would lodge in his memory bank.

I admired Coach K growing up. He was a guy who didn't have all the physical talent when he played basketball at West Point, but no one ever outworked him. In his career he has led his teams to four NCAA Championships, eleven Final Fours, and four Olympic gold medals ('84, '92, '08, '12). He was a coaching legend; it would give anyone goose bumps to play for him.

When I got to Durham in the summer of 2000, less than a month after graduating from high school, I made friends with incoming freshman point guard Chris Duhon. We bonded during one-on-one full-court pickup games. That summer I was able to build a relationship with the team. I made myself visible to the whole Blue Devil basketball staff, hanging around like some sort of hoops groupie. When the basketball team returned from Thanksgiving holiday after competing in the 2000 Maui Classic in Hawaii, they invited me to a practice. I never expected to play in a game that mattered. There were eight McDonald's All-Americans on that team (two still playing in the league today): Nate James, Shane Battier, Casey Sanders, Carlos Boozer, Jason Williams, Mike Dunleavy, Chris Duhon, and Nick Horvath. I figured the odds of my ever seeing court time were slim to none, but as of that November, I was an official walk-on. It was a deeply satisfying accomplishment.

I'll never forget the first day I practiced with the basketball team. Coach K held everyone to such a high standard. He was reviewing game tape and erupted over how the team wasn't going "hard enough," and singled out some of the stars for criticism. And this was from a game where Duke had *won* by a pretty a large margin. And yet the message was, "You're not physical enough, you know this isn't good enough. This is not championship basketball; we will not win a championship if we continue to play like this."

It was my introduction to Coach K's modus operandi: Always think about how to be your best regardless of who the opponent is. Be sure you can compete at the highest level against anyone, with the same effort and preparation for a championship game as you would have for a pre-season game. Be ready at all times. It was from Coach K that I first heard the phrase "Success is where preparation meets opportunity," a principle that resonated with how my parents had raised me.

Coach K believed that once you had the Duke jersey on, it was the same as wearing a bull's-eye on your back. You were carrying the reputation of Duke University on your shoulders. And he feared there would be people who believed they could extract value from that association at your expense. Coach K wanted anyone who intersected with a Duke player to limp away thinking, *Those guys are tough; they were there on every play; I never want to come up against those guys again.* Coach K never accepted mediocrity. Ever.

That work ethic was well-worn territory for me. When I was a child, my parents had taught me the value of pushing yourself beyond what you believed you could do. And I hated losing more than anything else. I was never one of those people who was "fine" so long as we had "played hard."

Just as with football, in a long stretch as a walk-on player for the basketball team I didn't see very much game time, if any. At practice I would guard Shane Battier. I went hard, but let's be real: I lacked size and talent. A six-foot-five eighteen-year-old up against a six-foot-nine Shane Battier. So practice was really about my getting educated in humility every day.

Well, almost every day. There was one shining moment during my first practice with the team in the '00–'01 season when the ball bounced off the rim and I dunked it back over Shane. There was almost a moment of silence in the gym. Followed by a few looks of disbelief.

He was captain of the team at the time. And I was a walk-on. And me dunking on him was akin to trying to date his sister. That move would not go unpunished.

That was the last play I made against him the entire season. From that moment on, Shane devoted every second of his remaining time at Duke to keeping me from scoring on him again.

(FYI: he never got over it. Ten years later, when Shane played for the President's forty-ninth birthday party round-robin tourney with LeBron, DWade, Kobe, and Chauncey Billups, he was still focused on shutting *me* down. By then he'd spent a decade in the NBA and earned hundreds of millions of dollars, but old grudges die hard. During one game where he was on the President's team, I was seconds from scoring when Shane, who wasn't even guarding me, ran at me like a bat from hell and blocked what I thought was going to be an uncontested layup. His voice echoed through the gym: "Anyone but Love!")

Outside of Shane burying me day in and day out, being a Duke walk-on was the opportunity of a lifetime. My abilities and knowledge of the game were improving exponentially with exposure to great players and coaches. (This happens in every field, at every level. No one progresses in a pool of folks just like them.) Then, during a game against Maryland, our center Carlos Boozer broke his fifth metatarsal, a bone in his foot. It was also the middle of spring football season. And, without any buildup, Coach K told me in the locker room, "Reggie, next game, we need you to play."

I was taken aback. I had spent my basketball life believing I would play on the perimeter. I didn't have anything like Boozer's build, height, or skill. But Coach K presented it as a flat choice: "You can see playing time as a forward or sit on the bench as a guard."

I played forward.

*　★　★

It was a steep learning curve. And I knew I was no Carlos Boozer. But, just as I had when I was tapped without warning to hit the football field, I went in and I did my best.

In both cases, stepping up was an unnerving test of my confidence and abilities. It was also far superior to the alternative: growing comfortable on the bench.

We are all quick to turn ourselves into victims, to protest that life isn't evenly balanced. Or complain that a teacher, coach, or supervisor is too harsh. Maybe they are—so what? They see something in you that they aren't getting out of you. It's good when your superiors hold you accountable to perform at a higher standard. It means they sense a potential that you haven't quite captured. It means that they see more for you than you do for yourself. Indeed, the time to get concerned is when people stop coaching you hard, when people stop expecting more of you.

The game Coach K called me in for was a game against UNC that would decide who won the ACC regular season—a game so hotly anticipated that tickets were going for almost $2,500 on Craigslist. I had no idea when or how much I was going to play. I was so keyed up about the *possibility* of playing in front of forty thousand spectators in the Dean Dome, my blood was pumping like a geyser. When I hit the floor, I was all over the place, like a raccoon on speed. It took a bit of time to work out that excess energy. Once I did, I pulled down a few rebounds and I defended the seven-foot Brendan Haywood. That felt incredible. I ended up on the court for five minutes, and we managed to pull out a win that many people thought we couldn't get without Boozer.

A theme in my life was emerging.

6

YOU ARE NEVER NOT REPRESENTING

Among the many lessons Coach K taught me was that no one is bigger than the team. He constantly expressed how the little things counted and every play mattered. Even the smallest plays were important: help-side defense and coming over to take a charge, or blocking a shot to ensure the opposition wasn't given easy baskets, or setting proper screens to get teammates open, or valuing every possession, or going after every loose ball and rebound and not waiting and expecting someone else to make a play that you could make. Because you never knew which plays would make the difference in a win or loss, you had to treat them all as if they carried the same weight.

Consistent play and stellar conditioning were Coach K's fundamental pillars. He also believed that any time you stepped onto the court the factors that were under your control—such as effort, defense, and knowing the scouting report and habits of key players on the opposing team—were all things you should have mastered. He understood that raw athleticism can only carry a team so far. He stressed that as a player for West Point, he was never the most talented player on the court, and neither was I at Duke. I was a utility player. Never the star. But we both loved to play. I didn't join the team because I believed I was going to enter the NBA and earn millions, though it would have been nice. I joined the team for the love of the game. And I think Coach K recognized that passion in me.

During my freshman year, I remember a particular game against Florida State. It was my first matchup against a former AAU rival and occasional teammate, Mike Joyner, who was a much taller and smoother player than I was, the sort of guy you would rather have on your team than have to defend against. During the middle of the game I made a shot at the rim, just laid the ball in the basket like a baby in a crib. The next day, with the team sitting in a U shape watching film of the game, Coach K said in his deadpan voice, "You know, Reggie, you can dunk the ball if you want." As if I were unfamiliar with the rules of collegiate basketball. My teammates' laughter only confirmed my intention to dunk the ball at the next opportunity.

One of the more moving things I witnessed while playing for Coach K was his desire to connect us with the military men and women serving in Iraq, to educate us about what real sacrifice looked like and to remind us of our shared good fortune. It was a reality check I sorely needed during my sophomore year, when I fell down the hole of despair after the most humiliating event of my life.

It happened when I was nineteen, right around the end of the ACC regular season. It was spring, so I had football workouts in the morning and basketball practices in the afternoon, attending classes in between. I was studying political science, but I didn't put much stock in my studies. I would log my B's, then check off the classes as one less thing I had to worry about. My desire to excel in the classroom had waned. I was consumed with being an athlete.

But the pursuit left me depleted. A part of every weekend was spent watching tape; every day I spent hours sweating in the weight room. It was constant. It sucked up a lot of my life, and as a result, on the weekends I chased the usual ways a stressed-out nineteen-year-old college sophomore blows off steam. Without a doubt, I drank more than I should have. Overall, I was stretched too thin. Earlier in the year, in a football game against Northwestern, I had pulled my hamstring. Instead of resting a few games, I played injured for the rest of the season at the suggestion of people I thought I trusted. As a result my production on the football field slowed to a halt for the remainder of the season and the team went on to another winless season. These dubious choices didn't improve my attitude. It left me clouded and pissed off.

Then, in February 2002, a good friend was celebrating his nineteenth birthday and asked me to join him and some pals at a fraternity party in Chapel Hill. I did, and long story short, I ended up passed out alone on a futon. I had no idea how long I was there, or what happened while I was unconscious.

I would soon find out.

It couldn't have been more than an hour after I awoke before I had friends emailing me with the subject line "Oh man, Reggie, what have you done?"

There were photographs attached to the emails. Pictures that had been emailed around UNC, Duke, and who knows where else, of me with random drunk dudes pretending to straddle my face. Then the photos hit the Internet. And in the click of a mouse, I was no longer the hardworking, two-sport athlete from Duke. I was the drunk at the frat party being pranked by even drunker guys with precious little shame. I vividly remember how livid Coach K was the day he brought those pictures of my passed-out butt on that green futon into the locker room before practice. I'd seen him empty lockers onto the floor, stacking all the gear in the middle of the room, yelling that we didn't deserve to wear the Duke uniform, that we weren't worthy of the equipment or the facility or the fans. I'd seen him so furious that he would say nothing at all. I'd known him too pissed to come to practice, letting the assistants run us for hours. But that day he seemed angrier than all those times combined.

He turned my humiliation into an example for the whole team. "You guys just don't get it. People see you, and they see the school." (And by "people," he meant rival UNC students who lived to punk any Duke player.)

He was holding the pictures of me in his hands, flipping through them, raging. "This is what some people want to do to you because you play Duke basketball." And then he turned to me and said, "What I'm trying to figure out is how you don't see just how lucky you are to be on this team."

It crushed me. I felt like I had let everybody down. Him. My parents. My teammates. I had been given an opportunity most people never get, and it looked like I didn't cherish the opportunity, that I was ungrateful or unaware of the privileged place I found myself in. I was not protecting the brand. I was tarnishing it. I went into the bathroom and did something I hadn't done since I was a kid: I broke down and cried.

And then, it got worse.

Over a weekend break, I spent a night in jail. I'd been pulled over late one night in Charlotte and been administered a Breathalyzer test. My old friend and I had been playing Madden NFL at his house, where we'd shared a couple beers each between us. After a couple hours, I left to get some donuts. Krispy Kremes, more precisely. They didn't have a Krispy Kreme in Durham, and I was craving some. I didn't think about the beers I'd had because I knew I wasn't intoxicated.

The Breathalyzer showed I wasn't over the legal limit. But I was underage, and North Carolina has a zero-tolerance policy for minors drinking, which meant that any blood alcohol level above zero was grounds for arrest. Out came the handcuffs. I couldn't believe it was happening. They took me in and booked me. It was nerve-wracking. A half hour later, I was in an empty cell, with no one on duty to process me out until the next morning.

It wasn't my best moment, but I was fairly sanguine about the arrest. After it happened, I didn't tell anyone. Not because I was afraid to, but because in my mind it really wasn't that terrible. I wasn't drunk. I hadn't wrecked my car or damaged property or injured myself or anybody else. I'd been caught drinking underage, been punished, paid my fine, and moved on.

But I'd forgotten that DUIs are public record. And after the party photos made the rounds, I discovered just *how* public.

My parents were clued in when my insurance bill skyrocketed a month later. I explained that it wasn't worth worrying about. They disagreed. They saw the DUI as a massive deal. They'd been giving me $200 a month in gas money. That promptly stopped. My mom, in particular, was concerned that I was drinking at all. Her father had been a fairly violent drunk. She wanted to know if I had "a problem with alcohol." She was worried about history repeating itself in the family.

After the UNC photos came out, I became a person of interest. As those shots circulated virally, people started looking at me more closely, and the DUI was unearthed and reported in the local papers. Which is how it came to the attention of the Duke coaching staffs, four months after the fact.

Mostly they were pissed that they had been caught off-guard. I got a call from Ben Reese, the dean of students, who ordered me into his office. Then the football coaches called me in right after that. The dialogue was identical.

"What do you have to say for yourself?"

"Well," I joked, "there goes my career in politics."

I was acting like a smart-ass. I didn't understand the gravity of the situation. In my mind, there were much worse offenses I could have been involved in, offenses college athletes are frequently being called on the carpet over. I didn't fight anybody. I didn't carry a gun. I wasn't using dope. I wasn't cheating on my academics. Never mind. With a DUI combined with my unfortunate impromptu photo shoot, it was determined that I had engaged in "conduct detrimental to the team." I was not being the Blue Devil steward I was supposed to be.

As punishment for my carelessness, I wasn't allowed to dress for games "indefinitely." The hiatus ended up being for the rest of the Duke basketball season. I couldn't even dress for the 2002 ACC tournament played in my hometown of Charlotte. I was that much of an embarrassment to the team. The only way I could do my part for Duke in the NCAA Sweet Sixteen was to cheer from my couch.

What I came to understand was that my photos of shame were not about me—though they certainly felt that way at the time. Because I was a basketball player on a storied team, I was always representing that history, even off campus at a friend's nineteenth birthday party at 2 A.M. When it came to Duke basketball, there were no days off from being an example to others.

Turns out I was lucky to receive that message early in life, during my sophomore year in college. It was the perfect tutorial for my time with the President. If there were ever a time when a man was symbolizing something larger than himself, it was as an African-American personal aide to the first African-American president. Screwing up in college had put me on alert: certain positions carry outsized responsibilities, and working for Obama meant my every move and word would be scrutinized. The choices I made about what to say, how to behave, whom to confide in, and where and with whom to spend my time would either tarnish or bolster the presidency.

This will always be the deal. No matter what I achieve in the future, I will never not be "Reggie Love, former aide to President Barack Obama."

Every misstep I make will be weighed against that title, and will reflect, rightly or wrongly, on the President. I may act alone, but the consequences extend much further. This can feel a bit burdensome, but from the beginning the bigger part of me was ready to rise to the occasion. In truth, no one on this planet walks without the weight of history, even if it is just your family name.

★ ★ ★

Going into my junior year at Duke, I became a different guy. Not as angry. Not as immature. I was beginning to see the bigger picture. It hit me that my football coaches were under more pressure to win games than I could fathom. They had taken up permanent residence in the hot seat. They could be fired at any minute, lose the economic security for their families. I'd been naïve about the business side of college sports, the crippling politics. Once I had that insight and realized I didn't know better than they did, I left all my self-involved nonsense behind, stopped bitching about the calls and the coaches' decisions. Ironically, it took getting wiser to grasp how little I actually knew.

By the time I was a senior, I'd figured out my place was working as an extension of the coaches. I knew I needed to act right to build culture. It took me a while, but I recognized that if I acted a fool, other players thought they could too. If I wanted everyone to win, I needed to fixate on myself less. So I organized players. I made sure we had continuity on and off the field. Younger teammates were looking up to me. I was a leader because I was seen as the older, more experienced guy.

In December of 2004, I was named the captain of the Duke basketball team. Coach K announced, "This season I am naming Reggie captain because he shows up every day regardless of what's going on off the court, personally or in his family. He walks on the court and plays the game the way it should be played. If everyone played the game like Reggie, we would win a national championship." It was one of the proudest moments of my life.

Getting appointed captain was the chance I'd been waiting for. It gave me an opening to rectify all the damage I'd done. To be a positive influence instead of a pariah. To show the other guys growth was possible—and necessary.

I'd gone from not good enough to make the squad to being the first walk-on/non-recruited player to both make captain and be a starter. I'd gone from embarrassing myself and my teammates to inching my way back through hard work and humility, finally letting go of the ego that had given me such a bad attitude that sophomore year. I had arrived in Durham thinking, *I got this, just give me the chance and I will excel.* I wasn't used to losing. I wasn't used to not playing. I had to be knocked down before I could climb higher.

There was something else that terrible year gave me. Another unexpected gift. And that was finding out what authentic friendship looks like.

When I was persona non grata on the team, so filled with self-loathing and unchecked rage, my then roommate Chris Duhon stood by me. He had been with me the night of the birthday party, when the photos were snapped and took my pride along with them. "I should have had your back," he said. "I let you down."

He didn't. But his sentiment filled me with unexpected solace. He was still in my corner. And so were many of my other teammates and friends. Nobody bailed. The Darryl Scotts, Erik Stowes, Andrew Moores, David Callaways—they stuck with me in the muck. Soon enough, it would be my turn to do the same. Only I would be doing it on a different playing field.

7

OWN YOUR MISTAKES

In the beginning, there was . . . awkwardness.

The two of us were usually packed tight in minivans, town cars, suburbans, small airplanes, casting about for things to discuss or reading in silence in preparation for the next round of events. Most of the time the senator would ask me questions I didn't know the answers to. About the schedule. About the briefings. I spent most of my first four months on the job saying, "Let me see if I can find out."

I sensed his disappointment. There were times when I wouldn't have the information he wanted, and I'd say, "I'll ask," and he'd say, "I'll just talk to them myself."

It wasn't a good look for me. Complicating matters, the senator was used to taking care of his own business. He wasn't about having help, especially help that was playing catch-up all the time. I began to have nightmares about someone saying to the candidate, "Reggie said he would get this done and he didn't!" I had pride in my job. I just didn't know what my job was yet.

I *did* know that early on he saw me as superfluous. At times, I believe I was a source of aggravation, a gnat he couldn't swat away. Let's just say, Obama and I went through a long and difficult "adjustment period."

And then, in the spring, just as the weather and the candidate were beginning to thaw ever so slightly, I committed the biggest screwup of my bodyman career to date.

It was April 26, 2007, three days before my twenty-fifth birthday. We were in Miami, Florida, and the campaign had just officially been assigned Secret Service.

Interesting side note: when you receive a Secret Service detail is determined by assessed "threat levels," aka how likely it is the candidate could get shot. Obama's threat levels were dangerously high, a reminder that crisscrossing the country with a black candidate for president carried unique risks. (Harry Reid said, jokingly of course, that the party couldn't afford to lose any Democratic senators given how slim its majority was.) Hence, early Secret Service detail.

We were in Florida to do a fundraiser with Cuban-Americans, hosted by Ricky and Eddy Arriola. The event had come up suddenly, so the schedule was more hectic than usual. The senator put his bag in the back of the Secret Service Suburban. We weren't staying overnight. Just a quick fundraiser and then an afternoon flight to South Carolina for the opening primary debate. It wasn't until the plane was in the air headed to Columbia that I noticed the candidate's bag was MIA. I'd never retrieved it from the vehicle.

The second I realized I'd forgotten the bag, my gut flipped. I knew instantly it was about as big a mistake as I could possibly have made. And I'd just made it.

It should be said that at this point in time, Obama was still very much about carrying his own belongings. He didn't like to exit a plane not holding anything. He would say, "JFK carried his own bags."

Nonetheless, the plane was airborne, the bag was missing, and I proceeded to have a full-blown panic attack. Sweat began to bleed through my clothes. My heart raced like a cornered rabbit. In my head I prayed he wouldn't notice, that I'd have time to find the bag and by some miracle get it back to him before he realized it had vanished.

In the meantime, I called Jessica Clark, then a finance assistant for the campaign, who in turn rang the Secret Service driver, who snagged the bag from the Suburban and drove it to Jessica, who handed it to a campaign member, who was flying to South Carolina to watch the debate. The bag was en route, at least. But we were going to beat it to the hotel by several hours.

When we landed in Columbia, I was feeling a modicum of relief, believing maybe disaster had been averted, maybe this would all resolve without any drama, and it was precisely at that moment that the candidate turned to me and said, "Hey, Reg, where's my bag?"

I froze, debating in my head whether to say "It's on the way" or "It's unavailable right now."

Obama, like most people, was not a man who enjoyed going without his personal effects. Especially not the Tumi containing his keys, his wallet, his credit cards, and everything he needed for the upcoming debate.

I went with, "It's on the way."

"What do you mean 'on the way'?" he asked, thinking I was joking.

"It's coming from Florida," I said, explaining how it had been left in the Suburban, but we had it, everything was fine, he'd have it in no time.

"You left my briefcase in Florida," he stated, incredulous.

And then: he said nothing. It was like I was back with Coach K, whose level of displeasure was inversely proportional to how little he spoke. The silence felt worse than being reprimanded.

As we rode to the Columbia campaign headquarters with Kirk Wagar without another word passing between us I thought, *That's it, I'm fired.* I kept hoping he would break the tension and yell at me. I was praying for that come-to-Jesus lecture; anything he could say would be better than not addressing the issue right then and there.

Once we arrived at the campaign field office, Obama asked for an office so the two of us could talk. We sat down at a circular conference table, face-to-face, no phones or computers. He began calmly.

"Listen, Reggie, I think you're a great guy."

Here it comes. Game over, I thought.

"But," he said and paused. There it was. The dreaded "but." I braced myself for the next line, and the candidate leaned forward slightly. "If you're not up to doing this job," he said flatly, "I can get someone else to do it."

I didn't know how to respond, so I kept mum while he continued talking, his voice even and firm.

"You have *one* job. And if I have to worry about all this stuff, then you're not making it easy for me to do *my* job."

It was like I was six years old and my dad was giving me a talking-to, only this was much worse because the father figure reprimanding me was trying to become the next President of the United States and my negligence had thrown a wrench into his efforts. I'd let the candidate down, he'd told me as much, and I felt nothing so much as ashamed.

I apologized. I told him he was right. I promised it would never happen again. There was nothing else I could do or say at that point. I couldn't undo my mistake. He just needed to decide if he could trust me. Which, thankfully, he did, and I was given another chance.

"Get your act together, Reggie. Help me do my job," he said, as he rose from the table and walked out of the room. I followed behind, chastened, and ran right into Marvin Nicholson, the former body-man for John Kerry and Obama's trip director, as well as a man who would become one of my best friends.

"What was that all about?" Marvin asked.

"I lost the bag."

He laughed a long, hearty laugh. "Yeah, that's happened to me before, when I worked for Kerry," he said, then added, "Seriously though, I wouldn't do it more than once."

Marvin was funny, even if he was half-Canadian. He stood six-foot-eight, and there was little he enjoyed more than giving me a hard time. Marvin took it upon himself to haze me until I was whipped into what he deemed some sort of shape.

Part of this was because when he was candidate John Kerry's bodyman, he was kept *busy*. Marvin would tell me stories about how hard he had it in the early days of email and cell phones, people still relying on fax machines and Filofax notebooks, and how his work-load of responsibilities had been exponentially greater. Whenever I would whine about anything I had to do for Senator Obama, Marvin was quick to shut my complaining down.

"You don't know how good you have it," he'd say, then walk away. He never helped me carry a single thing. It was a matter of principle. Once, Obama said to him, "Hey, Marvin, you going to help Reggie out?" And Marvin shook his head no.

"Reggie needs to earn his stripes. I've earned mine."

From that day forward I never asked Marvin for assistance with anything. Even if he tried to step in, I'd be clear: "*Don't* touch anything, I've got it." It became a point of pride.

Reflecting on this now, I understand Marvin's strategy. By mak-ing it a competition, he enabled me to have self-respect about parts of the job that were less than thrilling.

Near my twenty-eighth birthday three years later, Marvin handed me a present. It was a small wooden frame with a patch of military stripes displayed on the inside.

"I got it off eBay," he said with a grin. "You earned them."

★   ★   ★

I'm convinced the only reason Obama kept me on after the lost bag debacle was because I took full responsibility for leaving it behind. I did not blame the chaotic schedule or the Secret Service. I said it was my mistake. Simple as that. I'd seen Coach K do as much during my tenure at Duke. You would never hear him say to anyone that the team let him down. Instead he'd tell reporters, "I didn't have these guys ready to play. Any loss ultimately rests with me."

The senator was no different. He routinely accepted blame for the mistakes made by his staff. One example I recall vividly was the "D-Punjab" memo fiasco, where an interior correspondence was leaked criticizing Hillary Clinton's financial ties to Indian-American donors. When it accidentally went public, the candidate told the *New York Times* it was a "dumb mistake" and described the language as "unnecessarily caustic." He said he was ultimately responsible for the content of the document, even though he wasn't. (He hadn't even viewed the memo.)

Obama's willingness to swallow his pride and tarnish himself for the team rubbed off on me, and I didn't want to put him in a position where he had to do that for any mistakes I committed. So I redoubled my efforts not to make additional missteps. This is not to say there weren't other blunders. A page (or twelve) would go missing from a speech. Or the teleprompter would be busted, leaving it to the candidate to figure out how to improvise.

This happened at a Vegas Democratic Senatorial Campaign Committee fundraiser after he was president. He delivered a rousing speech, came off stage, jaw tight, and asked, "Sooooo, who forgot to put the rest of the speech in the book?"

"Excuse me, sir?" I said.

"After page ten, there was nothing."

We were like, "Oh, *man*." We scrambled. We had to figure out what had happened. It was like expecting your teammate to score without the ball.

"You couldn't tell from the performance," I offered, hoping that would soften the blow. It did not. At least this mishap didn't go down during the campaign, where every speech meant possible votes, and every error meant more intense negative coverage in the media. As the underdog in the race, the senator couldn't afford to come off looking like he didn't have his act together. He didn't have the benefit of history behind him. Or even the benefit of the doubt. He had to prove his worthiness at every stop.

During the 2008 campaign, the candidate worked off the stump, without formal remarks. A stump speech is basically the mainline pitch you deliver every day, to convince voters to support you. Obama would pepper the stump speech with local details. He did this effortlessly, his memory always a steel trap.

There was one morning in October when he was campaigning in Pennsylvania only a few weeks ahead of the election and the team had neglected to plan for bad weather. When I woke up, only a couple of hours before the call time of the first event, it was pouring out.

"Reggie, what's the rain site for this thing?" the senator asked me, eating his eggs and bacon.

There wasn't one. No rain site could accommodate a crowd this size, which I lamely tried to explain.

He pressed me. "So people are just going to be standing out in the rain and the cold waiting for me?" The idea of a crowd standing in a downpour didn't thrill him. Or me.

"I'm afraid they're already there, sir."

In fact, potential voters had been lining up in the wet for hours, like they were standing in line to get on the Ark.

Obama released a heavy sigh. "We can't have that."

"I know, sir. But it's too late to change the venue."

Obama dressed in casual "Iowa attire"—slacks and a windbreaker. He decided to break the schedule and go straight to the rally site and start the event as soon as possible so that people wouldn't be out in the rain and cold a minute longer than they needed to be. It was raining so hard that there were pools of standing water on the teleprompter screen, rendering it as useless as an inkless pen. Not only was he going to be speaking in a downpour, now he would be speaking in a downpour sans notes.

Nonetheless, the candidate came out to greet the voters with a big smile. He thanked everybody for enduring the miserable weather. He made a few opening remarks, then said, "I'm not going to keep you folks here long. I don't want you guys to be sick next week when I need you to get out and vote." You could hear the roll of laughter even over the din of the storm.

While the senator was giving his stump, I walked into the covered area where the rest of the staff was huddled, drinking coffee and staying warm. I gave one glance at them, glanced back at the crowd and Obama, and suggested it wouldn't be in anybody's best interest to be standing cozy and dry when the candidate finished the rope line.

Everyone glared at me. The weather was brutally cold and wet. (The same violent storm had also forced the cancellation of the World Series game in Philadelphia that day.) But they knew I was right. Down went the cups and out we went—all of us standing there, freezing and getting drenched in the deluge right along with him. Even in our misery, however, we picked up on the fact that something historic must be happening when several thousand people show up to see a presidential candidate in a torrential downpour.

I knew from the candidate that you don't jump ship when it gets rocky. Just as I learned from Coach K at Duke that you always have your teammate's back. You win as a team, lose as a team, you defend and rebound as a team—and never leave a man behind.

Obama slayed the speech, even without the teleprompter. The audience was pumped. He may have been unhappy about not having a better bad weather game plan and having to stand in a monsoon for half an hour, but it would have been much worse had his team not been united with him in the suffering.

Sports, politics, families—it's no different. When the rain hits the fan, you rally round your teammates. Just as in help-side defense in basketball—if your man has beaten you off the dribble, you have to trust that your teammate will step in to take the charge and protect the basket.

Everyone makes mistakes. Your turn will come. Remember to bring an umbrella.

8

LITTLE THINGS ARE BIG THINGS IN DISGUISE

If there was ever a role model for me in humility and class it was Pete Rouse. He was the guy who always worked as hard as every other person in the office and never made a fuss about anything. No job was beneath him. He handwrote letters. He returned every phone call. He never punted the crappy assignments. And he never claimed credit for the incredible work he *did* do. If there was internal strife, Pete would fix it. Between the DNC, the PAC, the campaign, the Senate, the House, and the presidency, he handled it all. He was the politician whisperer.

After I'd put together my early mail system, Pete came to me with a problem, needing my help. I was imagining some complicated systems request, or another data entry dilemma. We walked into his office, and he said, "I just got this new car. It has something called 'Bluetooth' and I can't seem to figure it out."

It was kind of funny, but his request also meant something to me. Of all the staff members in the entire office, I was the person he came to for help. I was just six months into the job. We had a professional IT guy on staff. But Pete picked me. I took it as a show of trust. After I set up his Bluetooth, he would travel around the office telling everyone he saw, "This kid is awesome! He can fix anything!"

Later, when Pete would introduce me to folks, he would announce, "The reason we hired Reggie is because Coach K said there was no task too small for him." That was why I got the job. Not because I went to Duke, or was a two-sport athlete. But because I understood what teamwork really meant.

★   ★   ★

I figured out early on in my athletic career that there is only one basketball. Everyone can't shoot a three-pointer on every play. Everyone can't be J. J. Redick. Someone has to do the unsexy stuff—setting screens, rebounding, defense, taking charges. Because I was never the star, that person was usually me. In football, I did much the same, acting as a downfield blocker and as a receiver. I understood that the less flashy, small jobs weighed as heavily in securing victory as a dunk or a touchdown. You can't have the latter without the former.

In a similar vein, the more mature I grew, the more I trusted my coaches. If they told me something was important, I believed them. I didn't need to know why. This learned willingness to care about the minutiae served me well as a bodyman, because minutiae and doing what the boss says are pretty much your whole existence.

Back in 2006, one of my earliest jobs at the senator's office was taking calls from constituents. To put it nicely, a lot of the callers were a little out of touch with reality. People who hated Democrats. Who hated people of color. Who believed all the vitriol coming from right-wing talk radio and television about Obama being a socialist, a Muslim, a terrorist among us. I had to be calm in the face of their hostility, basically talk them off the ledge.

Other callers were just lonely. They wanted someone to hear them. These folks called repeatedly. It got to where I could recognize some of their voices before they even said their names.

Once the senator announced his intention to run, on February 10, 2007, I transitioned from calls to finding office space and furniture. I traveled all over Washington, checking out every available location—tracking down who owned the building, how much the rent was, how long we could lease the property for, if and when we could scale up, how many more units we could take over. In a nutshell, I did whatever I could to keep Pete and the team telling the candidate I was a smart hire.

In truth, I was intimidated by the notion of helping to manage a presidential campaign. I was basically learning something new every day, though I did take some comfort in the fact that I wasn't the only one. As the candidate himself said to us on more than one occasion, "We are building this plane together as it's taking off down the runway."

Obama's typical day started early. Which meant I would get up thirty minutes earlier so I could: pack my bag, check emails and respond to the critical ones, check voice mail, make an abridged version of the day's schedule, and make sure the candidate woke up and got to a gym with enough time to work out *and* not be too late for the first event. Early on I was also responsible for figuring out his breakfast. This meant that no matter where we were, I had to find a place that made eggs, wheat toast, and bacon before sunrise. Then I had to bring the food back to wherever we were staying, trying to time my delivery so the meal wasn't cold by the time he was ready to eat, which I eventually got down to a science. But it started off as an experiment I was woefully unskilled at executing.

There were times when I felt a little like *What am I doing here?* I mean, I knew it was *something*, but I didn't know exactly what yet. The nuts and bolts of the work weren't innately inspirational. No one graduates from college and dreams of a career in bacon delivery. But the bigger picture was mind-blowing. And every day along in the campaign, it became easier to see how big that picture might actually become.

It was in the spring of 2007, after a visit to St. Louis at which Senator Obama lost track of the time while he was on the treadmill, that Marvin took me aside and advised:

"From now on, you go with him." "You think I liked biking at 6 A.M. with Kerry? If I could do that when I was thirty years old, it should be easy for you at twenty-five years old."

From that day on, I would dress in my exercise clothes and show up outside the senator's hotel room at the advised time for the gym departure and then wait there until he came out. Some days, when he was late, I would knock to make sure that the gym was still on the agenda. And some days he'd holler back, "Ten more minutes," which could turn into twenty. Against that possibility, I learned to take a pillow, prop it against his door, and go back to sleep until he emerged.

At the gym, we each had our own routine. Sometimes he would need a spot. Other times the TV would be on and the candidate would say, "Did you see this play last night?" The talk was generally about sports or pop culture. It was a nice break from the campaign.

Most of the facilities we used were terrible. Usually a squeaky treadmill and a couple of inoperable machines. The senator still committed to breaking a sweat every day for at least an hour. We'd share our exercise philosophies. I liked push-ups and sit-ups. He preferred weight training. Sometimes he would ask me how I used to bulk up in between basketball and football season.

In cities and hotels that we would visit routinely, like the Airport Hampton Inn in Des Moines, Iowa, it was a small victory to know that there was a gym less than two blocks away that actually had legit equipment. Obama appreciated being able to use seventy-pound dumbbells, a squat rack, or adjustable benches. And the fact that there was a Perkins open early enough for breakfast that shared a parking lot with the hotel? Like winning the lottery.

Those early gym hours seemed trivial on the surface, but they were key to surviving the rigors of the campaign. Everyone loves to win games, but most people hate conditioning. They forget that conditioning is what puts you in a position to win the close games.

At first, the workouts were just another item on the morning's list, along with emails and abridged schedules. But they did allow us to interact in a more relaxed setting. You were never unaware of the campaign, but when we were working out, it receded a bit. The experience was normalizing. And like installing the Bluetooth for Pete Rouse, the exercise routine was a big thing disguised as a small thing. It showed that I was along for the journey. Every sweaty step of it.

9

TOSS OUT THE PLAYBOOK

At Duke, as the debacle that was 2002 and my sophomore year lurched on, I called the wide receiver coach from UCLA, since they had recruited me in high school. I was looking into transferring schools. Our starting QB wasn't returning to the team because of academic challenges. I'd weathered a shitty semester and a shitty football season. Given all that had happened, getting out of Dodge seemed like a good idea. I'd never lived outside the South. And I started to think that now was the time.

My father had become ill. He'd been sick most of the academic year, but then he took a scary turn and was admitted to the hospital at Duke. His eyes had swollen shut. His motor skills were failing. The doctors were initially at a loss. After a month, he was diagnosed with a rare respiratory virus.

His illness shook me to my foundation. My father had always been my rock, steadfast and invincible. Present at every game. Leading me through the crosshairs of life. As he was waylaid in a hospital cot, I was spending much of my time running around playing sports. For the first time I deliberated, *What am I actually doing with my life?* When time with someone you love stops being a guarantee, you begin to examine how you spend the hours you do have. Did I even want to continue to play sports?

One night, I shared with him my plan to transfer and move to California. And my dad said, "Look, I don't know how long I'm going to be healthy. And I definitely won't be able to travel out to California to see you play."

In all my self-absorption about the commotion surrounding Duke, I hadn't thought about what it would mean to leave my family. I knew my dad wanted me to stay close to home, in case the worst happened and my mom needed me. But he also wanted his son to finish what he'd started. He didn't want me to be a quitter just because I'd faced some adversity.

He was home by then, but I remembered him in his hospital bed, this six-foot-one, 240-pound stoic giant of man leveled so suddenly, and I knew what he desired was a small ask. Even in that weakened state, he was guiding me, reminding me what was really important. Family. Seeing my commitments through to the end. Rising up, not scurrying away. My father had bent over backward for me my whole life. Not running off to California was the least I could have done for him. So I stayed.

After six weeks, my dad was released from the hospital. But his brush with death left me deeply unnerved. I found myself exploring parts of my psyche that I'd previously ignored in favor of pursuing athletics. All my life I'd wanted to be a professional athlete. But what if there was something more?

That summer I decided—somewhat spontaneously—that I

was going to head to Indiana to work for secretary of state candidate John Fernandez. I was majoring in political science and public policy, but I knew nothing about the intricacies of a statewide campaign. It was my first official dip into politics. And my first extended stay away from everyone and everything familiar. Much to my shock, I loved every minute of it. I'd met John Fernandez, the mayor of Bloomington, Indiana, through Alan Hogan. When I met John, I liked him immediately. He was smart, progressive, full of passion. Part of my job was to canvass with the candidate and speak to people all over Indiana, to find out the issues the constituents cared about. Sometimes we talked sports, but more often I was drawn into conversations about social policy, day care, minimum wage, health insurance, the effect of daylight saving time on livestock. I spent my days exchanging ideas and listening to folks I would never have spoken to before. I also traveled as an aide to Fernandez for specific events and fundraisers, depending on who was hosting and who the guests were. Indiana is not what I'd call the most progressive state in the union, but during the campaign there were appearances during which it made strategic sense to display some diversity—aka me. I didn't mind being "the diversity." Being a new kind of role model came naturally. And let's be honest: Hoosiers love basketball.

I remember walking with the candidate, a man not a lot of people knew much about, touring alien cities, getting water when he was thirsty, handing out literature, keeping pace side by side as we marched in Fourth of July parades in places like Fort Wayne and Gary. I was experiencing new territories literally and figuratively. I was well out of my comfort zone, in an atmosphere where my physical abilities were irrelevant. My brain was alive. I felt stimulated and tuned in to a world bigger than my own, and certainly bigger than athletics, which was all I knew.

The people I worked with on the campaign were also a new breed to me. They were dynamic and fervent about making Indiana a better place. I saw how one person, even in a lowly position, could make a measurable difference in the outcome by contributing his or her best effort for the team, and I became even more impressed with John's will to win. And I assumed everyone else was too. I was confident we would win the election.

That Indiana gang taught me more than just how a local campaign was managed. I recall one weekend, as I was driving to an event with a couple members of the group, when my ex-girlfriend called. Lydia Guterman was a smart and beautiful woman who constantly pushed me to be better personally, athletically, and academically. She was about to be a senior at the University of North Carolina as a Morehead Scholar and had seen the world by age twenty-one. Lydia and her parents, Wylly and Jim, always treated me like I fit in and belonged even when I didn't. Lydia had recently shared that she had started dating women. She rang to tell me that she was traveling to D.C. for her first LGBT march.

"Why would you waste your time on that?" I said glibly.

"Seriously?" she snapped back at me. "Is that your actual opinion?"

"Yeesssss," I said, unsure of why she was so tweaked. I was at the age where I thought the only things that were important were things that *I* did.

My ex spent the next twenty minutes educating me on the value of activism and of fighting for your rights, and, perhaps most vociferously, explaining in minute detail why I was being a Grade A jerk.

When I hung up the phone, my new campaign pals were oddly quiet.

"What?" I asked. "Not you guys too?"

My friend Alan gently suggested that maybe I should rethink my perspective. "Try and understand what is important to other people even if you don't understand why it is. Listen first, and endeavor to be respectful."

That landed with me. It didn't matter if I wasn't invested in my ex-girlfriend's cause. *She* was. It was a big move forward for me in developing some emotional intelligence. And though I didn't know it then, it was good preparation for the future, when the concerns of an entire nation would become peripherally my business. My boss would need to listen with empathy to every single one of them—and by extension, I would too.

★ ★ ★

The Indiana campaign was in full swing when I had to return to Duke for football training camp. The fact that I had given up any part of the summer for something other than training in Durham had struck some of my coaches as breaking a fundamental rule of the playbook. So, as much as I hated to leave, my Duke commitment was calling. Then, as life tends to do, it threw me a curveball in the form of a knee injury, MCL and PCL tears—you have a better chance of winning the state lottery than tearing both those ligaments. Less than a month before the Indiana election in October, and I was out for the year in both sports.

My coworkers from Indiana, Angie Gates and Lori Lambert, who had become good friends, sent a "Get Well" balloon bouquet to my apartment. I was touched. The injury came in the middle of the season and when I was one of the top receivers in the ACC for yards and catches, and my coworkers were among the few to truly appreciate what a blow it was. Of course, I was bummed to be sidelined. But I wasn't as demoralized as I'd been about previous injuries. I was beginning to understand how life goes off script. Things may not happen the way you want them to. And the true test of character is how you respond when they don't.

In the end, John Fernandez lost the election. He put together a well-run, well-financed effort. Turnout was strong. His support was visible and vocal. He outraced his opponent in every measurable way, and still lost. He was sidelined by fate, just like me.

It was after his loss that I fully recognized how much I'd evolved that summer I spent in Indiana. I'd witnessed the uncertainties of the political culture. How unpredictable it can be. How exciting. I'd learned how to communicate more effectively and to invest in the concerns of people outside of my circle of understanding. I'd embraced emotions beyond anger and disdain. I'd seen that I was more than a point on a scoreboard. And I realized that the final score isn't always the whole truth of the game.

That summer ended up being the start of an entirely new path in my life. The pivot point that would take me on a completely uncharted course. And I would never have stumbled onto it if I hadn't thrown out the playbook.

10

COURT CONNECTION

Tramping through New Hampshire in the dead of winter redefines cold.
It feels like you are packed in ice and someone turns a fan on. There
are no major highways that run east to west, and the north-south
roads are serpentine, so travel takes hours more than you'd like it to,
which means you stay cold longer. For a Southern guy like me, it was
no picnic. But what I recall even more than the freezing temperatures
is that New Hampshire was the place where Obama and I first started
playing hoops together.

I like to believe that learning to handle my responsibilities as his
personal aide earned me Barack Obama's trust, but I also know that
the strength of our friendship grew out of our shared love of basketball. Our age difference meant we were on different cultural pages,
and in different life stages, but basketball was the common ground

we could come together on. Hoops was also something we could talk about that didn't drain him the way his other daily conversations could. Sports permitted him to escape the grind of the campaign, and it was an icebreaker. Basketball modified the tenor of our interactions and took us from boss and underling to something more like friends. It began with the 2007 NBA playoffs.

I'll never forget the night I got an email in my inbox from the candidate consisting only of Tony Parker's stat line.

I chuckled, then typed back, "Those are good numbers. But it was against a weak team." Then I added Chris Paul's stat line.

And with that little exchange, something just shifted in our relationship. The communication didn't involve a to-do list or a complaint or a question about the schedule. It was purely fun. And spoke of a touch of competition between us. Who was going to be right? The debate went on for years. (After Chris Paul won All-Star Game MVP in 2013, Obama conceded, reluctantly.) Though Tony Parker's NBA championship ring collection (four in all: 2003, 2005, 2007, and 2014) may make the President's case for him a little better than mine for Chris Paul. A discussion for a later date, though.

It was Matt Rodriguez, then state director for New Hampshire, who first suggested we should shoot hoops on the campaign. He thought it could help build relationships. Clinton had a throttlehold on the state. The logic was basic: If you don't find a way to connect with voters, you have very little chance of earning their support. But if you can connect with them, there's a chance they'll like you and carry that enthusiasm back to their organizations.

It was a solid idea. For me, playing H-O-R-S-E or playing in pickup games was something I lived for, it energized me. You'd come away feeling good about the run, as long as you didn't get your butt kicked. Basketball was also a true passion for the candidate, similar to how it was for my college coach; on the court he was a guy you wanted to play with, and he always made anyone he played with better. Hoops was also a natural way for people to get a window into the candidate as I knew him.

Obama loved the idea of connecting with the locals through sports. As a former community organizer, he knew the value of that kind of informal interaction, how it built bridges and made connections with people who, typically, would have been the least likely to support him.

Our first on-court event was with local New Hampshire firefighters. We were barely into the game when it became clear it was going to be a rout. We were burying them.

After I had managed to steal the ball and take it for a quick layup, the senator walked over to me and said, "Reggie, we want to win. But we also want to win their support."

I was twenty-four, just over a year from having trained with the Dallas Cowboys. And no one had ever coached me to play at half speed. My competitive instincts didn't have a lower gear.

"Let's just settle down a little bit," the candidate whispered, passing me the ball.

It was a tricky balancing act. It didn't help the senator if we played too well and it looked like we came in with a bunch of ringers. But it also didn't serve the campaign if we played and lost. The ideal scenario was to win gracefully, without humiliating the opposition. This is not to say that games were thrown, but there wasn't a lot of dunking by our team when we played with future voters.

When we started playing basketball just among the campaign team and our friends, it was a very different story. Obama's initial directive was straightforward: "No one takes it easy on me."

So we didn't. We all played full-on, no mercy. (This worked great until, after the election, the President took an elbow from another player that resulted in him getting more than a dozen stitches in the lip, and the first lady promptly reminded him, "You aren't twenty years old.")

Mrs. Obama had a point; the leader of the free world shouldn't be showing up to press conferences with black eyes, random bruises, or on crutches. In my years of playing competitive sports, I've sprained both ankles, fractured teeth, dislocated fingers, gotten staples in the head, stitches in my arm, torn my MCL and PCL, broken my foot, torn a hamstring, torn ligaments in my fingers, received stitches in my chin twice, the second time in 2010 during a game of hoops with the President.

That injury was courtesy of my older brother, Richard Love Jr.— though his high school friends nicknamed him Sleepy, because his eyes looked like those of a pot smoker. Richard, a beautiful gospel singer and a gifted scholar, has always been an exceptionally smart guy; as a seventeen-year-old he would beat our parents at *Jeopardy*. He was innately better than me when it came to the classroom, so he owned the category of academics. I remember my parents wishing my academic performance were a fraction of his. But I was into sports; in high school that is where I distinguished myself.

The day Richard sent me to the White House ER was the Saturday morning prior to the annual White House Correspondents' Dinner, which is like the Political Academy Awards. He was living with me at the time, working in D.C. for NOAA, the National Oceanic and Atmospheric Administration, and had been needling me about wanting to join a game. Usually when he asked to play in the morning games I would say no, explaining, "The guys I play with get up at 5 A.M. to hoop. They've all played in college. These guys want to win. They are not okay with losing." He didn't understand. His feelings were hurt. So on the morning of the dinner, I relented, and he joined us on the court.

An hour into the game, my brother was guarding someone coming off a screen I was setting, when he turned to get through my screen and slammed his forehead into my chin. The skin split on impact. Blood sprayed everywhere. It looked like an NBA-themed episode of *CSI*.

The President jogged over to inspect the damage.

"Whoa!" he said, shuddering. "Well, you know, Reggie, I have to admit, it's better you than me."

The game was called, and I was shuttled to the White House, where Dr. Ronny Jackson gave me fifteen stitches. I still made it to the dinner. I wore a bandage under my chin to keep the blood from dripping onto my tux. The President could only chuckle when he saw me prior to the event.

★ ★ ★

Even though playing basketball was a thousand times more fun than anything else we did on the campaign, we were never allowed to substitute a game for an event. Games were viewed as "add-ons." If Obama could have substituted a game for a town hall, nine out of ten times he would have said, "Let's hoop!" Instead, he'd do several town halls and try and squeeze in court time before, at like 5:30 or 6 A.M.

Off the court, we'd do what felt like an endless number of house parties a day. There would be events at community centers, group homes, university campuses, and retirement homes, along with stops at every mom-and-pop diner to ask customers for their support.

Obama would stand up and introduce himself, explain why he wanted to be president, why he thought he'd make a good leader. And then he would open the room to questions. They were usually about local issues, which were often politically complex and toxic.

There were a lot of concerns about his age: "You seem awfully young." "Are you seasoned enough for the highest office?"

He'd unpack his history of Chicago politics, point out they were as rough as anywhere. He'd argue that his short history in the Senate freed him from years of baggage, grudges, and the rain checks old-timer incumbents inevitably owed to their base of supporters and their colleagues. He believed his newness to the game would make him more effective, not less.

I wouldn't sit during these events. I stood off to the side or toward the rear of the room. I needed to be ready, but not intrusive. Seen and not heard. Like a child in Victorian England, if that child were six-foot-five and carrying a Tide stain remover pen. The most important thing was having eye contact with the candidate all the way from the back of the room, so that I could cue him when we were out of time.

"Sir, you have time for one more question," I'd say. Then we'd leave the event and go do the whole thing again.

When I reflect on that time in my life, the word that most often pops into my head is "crazy." Obama was logging four, five, six, seven campaign stops a day. Hillary? Maybe she was doing two or three. At most. Ours was not a typical campaign. We fought hard. And we played hard. Especially on primary days, when we played pickup games.

The tradition started in Iowa on January 3, 2008. It had been Obama's idea. A bunch of people had come in for the caucus, and the senator suggested that since we couldn't campaign on voting day—it was against the rules for a candidate to show up at a precinct—we should get a game together.

We did, playing with staffers, Secret Service, friends who flew in from Chicago, and lo and behold, we won Iowa.

The day of the New Hampshire primary, we didn't organize a game, and we lost. From then on, every election day in every state, we played basketball. It was a bit eerie. When we skipped Nevada, we lost there, too. The candidate and the team grew very superstitious. "Primary day? We're playing." End of debate.

As much as I loved hoops, Marvin hated it. But we were often short a player, so he'd have to lace up. The same way you have to play golf with your boss even if you'd rather not.

One day in Milwaukee, the candidate was speaking at a high school. He was dribbling a ball offstage. We'd played earlier in the day, and the competitive energy of the court was still alive. I said to Obama, "You know that's a girl's ball you're dribbling, right?" And he said, "Yeah, I know." Then he tossed the ball to Marvin and said, "Hey, maybe this will help your game."

It was meant in fun, but, ruffled, Marvin strutted over to the senator.

"With all due respect, I will take you to the hoop. I will beat you," he said. "Reggie might be able to take me one-on-one, but sir, there is no way you could beat me."

Obama pushed back, calling Marvin out on missing multiple crypts when we played on Super Tuesday. I felt like I was back in school, watching my teammates go at it on the playground.

"At least I didn't get my shot blocked by a fourteen-year-old boy," Marvin cracked.

"He was fifteen," Obama snapped back without hesitation.

Just as the candidate was about to open his mouth again and permanently shut Marvin down, the announcement came over the loudspeakers, "And now, here he is, the next President of the United States, let's welcome Senator Barack Obama!"

The candidate was mid sentence in his response to Marvin as the noise of the crowd hooting and applauding swept over us, and without missing a beat Senator Obama took the stage.

Later, he said to me that all he could think about during the speech was how fired up he was at Marvin thinking he could beat him in basketball. I could only laugh.

The series of games on primary days took place just about two years after I had moved into my crummy apartment on Capitol Hill. The senator and I had come a long way since our chilly beginnings. We'd gotten to know each other beyond boss and assistant. By then, there was trust, even friendship. Basketball provided something additional, something that went beyond the campaign. For two years he had observed my work ethic. He'd seen me own my mistakes and learn from them. On the court, however, he saw my desire to win. He also saw my love of the game, my commitment to it, which mirrored his own.

This new bond was never more tested than when we joined forces to coach Sasha's team of nine- and ten-year-old girls on how to pick and roll (well, to be honest, we were happy if they just set the pick).

The official coach of Sasha's team was Lisa Horowitz, a researcher from NIH and the mom of one of the players. She was a very congenial coach, but although she was a former college athlete in two other sports, her previous basketball experience went all the way back to high school varsity. The girls were in fourth grade, nine years old, and had some basic skills, but needed a little more structured guidance. Sometimes they were uncertain where to pass the ball or when to shoot. They needed to learn some tried-and-true plays.

The president would go to the games, watching with a running commentary to Michelle: "They should be playing a zone," or "They need to run a play on offense." After listening to him grumble about the situation, Michelle finally said, "Why don't *you* teach them how to play basketball?"

"Fine," he said. Next thing I knew, we were coaching girls' basketball.

When we met the girls on the court, I realized that as talented and smart as we thought we were about basketball, and life in general, teaching fourth graders the art of hoops was like herding cats; correction—herding giggling cats.

Like the President, I was used to sharing the court with players who loved the game and played with skill. These nine-year-olds would throw the ball over their teammate's head, directly out of bounds, and then just laugh about it. It was tough to convince them there wasn't anything funny about turnovers or air balling a shot seven feet from the basket.

In these circumstances the powers of the President's office were useless, but he had all the powers of an engaged and interested parent. He would see me getting frustrated and would interject himself, telling the girls firmly, "This is not a slumber party. You have to run hard, throw the ball hard, stand tall and be strong. You have to listen to your coach."

During the basketball season, Obama and I were actually courtside for a few games, he as head coach, me as his assistant. Michelle would come to cheer on the team.

We came to see that while Sasha's team might not love the mechanics of the game, like everyone else on the planet, they *hated* losing.

One afternoon we played the best team in the league. It was a tight score, head-to-head the whole time. During the competition I couldn't help myself and started shouting at the referee, trying to force a call to go our way. And then it happened: our team perfectly executed the pick-and-roll. We pulled out a 12–10 squeaker! Hysteria all around!

What coaching those girls, playing with constituents, and sharing the court with Obama revealed to me was that nothing connects people like athletics. Being on the same team wipes away all pretense. It gets to what's real, real fast. You feel what it is like to be a part of a bigger organism. You invest in other people. You work hard. You net measurable gains. Sports accomplishes all of this, whether you are tossing a ball in the backyard, swishing three-pointers in the league, or clapping like a maniac for a group of little girls as they race down the court.

11

DRESS THE PART

I began my stint as bodyman dressing in a half-dozen wrinkle-free, wash-and-wear dress shirts from Jos. A. Bank. I paired them with cotton pants and a few business-standard neckties you'd forget two seconds after you saw them. My humdrum wardrobe was a source of great amusement for my friends, especially my old college roommate and close friend Chris Duhon, who was playing point guard for the Chicago Bulls while I was learning the ropes on the Obama presidential campaign trail.

Whenever we landed in Chicago, Chris would let me crash at his place on North Kingsbury Street. His apartment became my second home. I did my laundry there. I was able to get my best meal of the week, prepared by Chris's chef at the time, Bryan Stotland, or, as everyone called him, B-Money. I would joke with Chris that if it weren't for B, he'd eat McDonald's three meals a day; I know during the campaign I ate there at least five times a week, and in some of the towns, it was considered fine dining. At Chris's apartment, I could spend time with friends who weren't involved in the Democratic primary. It was my periodic oasis.

Every Sunday watching me hanging up and stretching out my wrinkle-free Jos. A. Bank button-downs, Chris would crack up.

"Shit, man, those are some wrinkled-ass shirts."

I'd explain that when they air dried, the wrinkles would fall out. He'd just keep laughing. "Tell yourself whatever you have to, but that shit is wrinkled."

I think he felt sorry for me. So, on my twenty-fifth birthday, on April 29, 2007, Chris had his tailor Jamal Ali make me a suit, along with some dress shirts and elegant matching ties. The clothes were a step up to say the least, immaculately fitted and undeniably high class. He'd given me a man-style makeover. And people noticed. Even the candidate.

"I like that tie," Obama said the first time he saw me in my new suit. "I may want to wear that at some point." (He ended up borrowing it for the YouTube debate three months later.)

Although he is undeniably a self-possessed, detail-oriented man, the senator did not necessarily start his political odyssey worrying too much about his attire. He could even be, at times, sartorially challenged. Axelrod and Plouffe had to wean him off wearing his Black-Berry on his belt like a beeper. He had a fondness for donning the same pair of dress shoes for every event.

There was this one particular suit folks on the staff hated. It was the suit without any love, except from the candidate. Until the day it sort of got "left behind" in New Hampshire.

We were at a house event, and the senator was engaging the focused crowd as he always did, passions running high. The room grew warm, so he removed his suit jacket, whereupon the host of the event hung it in her coat closet. Where it stayed. For a couple of days.

Of course the candidate noticed immediately that the jacket was MIA. But no one knew where it had gone. Or at least they weren't saying they did. There was a lot of: "Where's the jacket?" "I think Marvin must have taken it." "I thought you had the jacket." "Do you have the jacket?" It was like an *SNL* "Really!?!" skit. We were all hoping the jacket would never materialize, no one more than Robert Gibbs, who had teased the candidate about evolving his look.

By the time the jacket was reunited with its pants, I think the senator had gotten the message about the suit.

Unlike other campaigns, our candidate didn't have a wardrobe consultant or stylist. More often than not, that job fell to me. He would dress, and then ask my opinion. I think this was less because he valued my take on fashion and more because I was the only person around. There was really no one else to ask.

"Looking sharp," I'd say, or, "Your tie's a little off." And if this was ahead of a debate or a major speech, we'd fist bump before he hit the stage.

I also filled the role of traveling valet. During the March primaries we made a stop at Penn State, where the candidate spoke in front of a crowd of a hundred thousand potential voters and a few cows. Before the candidate went to the rally site for the speech, the plan was to stop and visit the agriculture facilities on campus (fancy way of saying let's go visit a farm). We were in Central Pennsylvania and it would have been a shame to come all that way and not visit a dairy farm or two. We were advised to be prepared, and so I had been put in charge of procuring boots for the candidate.

The challenge was that the stop had been added to the schedule after the Sunday night stop in Chicago—where the candidate would replenish and refresh his wardrobe. Which meant when he packed for the week, no one had factored in pasture-appropriate footwear. As usual, the senator had an idea of how he wanted to look for the event, so as we headed into town, I phoned several shops, ordering a bunch of pairs in different sizes, 11, 11.5, trying to find the perfect boot with the perfect fit and look. Anytime the wardrobe changed from the typical slacks or suits with the black Kenneth Coles, he and the senior staff would quickly say, "We don't need any Dukakis moments," referring to the time presidential candidate Michael Dukakis wore an oddly sized soldier's helmet, resulting in a photograph that was used to ridicule him as soft on defense.

Shoes were always the biggest challenge for the senator. Shoes and ties, but mostly shoes. The man was particular about his feet. He wouldn't just throw on any old pair of mukluks. They had to look a certain way, feel a certain way. Anytime he couldn't wear his favored dress flats, it was an issue. (In certain photographs you can see that those shoes practically have holes in the soles from all the campaigning he did in them.) Throughout the campaign, I was always trying to scratch and scrounge to procure the ideal footwear. I'd send screenshots to the advance teams and say, "Find these!" Also, "Buy wool socks!" When I finally did find a pair of boots for Penn State that he loved—light brown Timberland steel-toes—I kept them on the plane for the duration of the campaign, just in case any surprise farm visits managed to find their way onto the schedule.

In the case of both myself and the senator, the clothes didn't necessarily make the man, but they did make a vital and intractable impression. We both had to learn how to dress the part. Because the impression we made could mean the difference between a yes or a no vote. Between respect and dismissal.

The same is true in any job.

You may not be representing your country, but you are representing your brand, your parents, your people. So shave. Shine your shoes. Iron your suit. Clean your face. You don't have to be Drake courtside with the lint roller, but by all means, control what can be controlled, so when things go awry, you at least look like you have it together. Good manners and self-respect will take you places money never can.

12

THERE'S NO PLACE LIKE HOME (COURT)

In January of 2004, at the age of twenty-one, I took remote classes and an independent study so that I could leave Duke for the winter/spring semester and train with Tom Shaw in New Orleans in preparation for my NFL Pro Day. I decided I needed to find out once and for all if I could ever have a serious football career, and I committed those months to getting into draft-day shape.

I booked a one-way flight to Louisiana alone. I packed only a few changes of clothes. When I landed, I went straight to Walmart, where I bought a cheap bike that I could use to get around. This wasn't because I loved cycling so much. I just didn't have the funds to buy, insure, and fuel a car, period. Most of what money I had was going toward room, board, and training. Mine was to be a focused, frugal existence. It would also be the first time I lived by myself in a city where I only knew one other person.

I trained four hours a day—two hours in the morning and two hours in the afternoon. The rest of my time was my own. The freedom was eye-opening. When you are a college-level athlete, your day is not only full, but also monitored. Between meals, meetings, classes, and workouts, virtually every hour of my time at Duke had been structured. In New Orleans, though, I was the master of my schedule.

I did some schoolwork. I walked the city. I explored every inch of the Metairie suburb of New Orleans. I would bike to the Esplanade Mall and go to the movies alone in the afternoon. I taught myself to cook. Chicken and potatoes, mostly. I ate crawfish. I watched Mardi Gras parades. I soaked up the live music, dancing alone.

I still had my apartment in Durham. My roommates would phone and say I was missing this great night or a blowout party. I'd say I wished I was there too. But I really didn't. I kind of enjoyed being away. It taught me I could do things on my own. It made me sit with myself and think. Who did I want to be? What did I want to do? What really made me happy and fulfilled? What happens if and when you make it? What happens if you don't? Questions I had never been forced to consider before, as I was always on to the next practice or game.

In New Orleans, I experienced life at a different pace. I had gone to test my affection and ability for a life in the NFL, but what I uncovered was far deeper than that. I discovered myself.

Then, toward the end of my tenure at the combine training clinic, my grandmother Elise passed away from complications due to Alzheimer's. My mother called to give me the news. She was sobbing.

I had spent every summer of my childhood at my grandmother's house in Mount Pleasant, South Carolina. I'd always remembered it as the most carefree time of my youth. My grandmother loved her

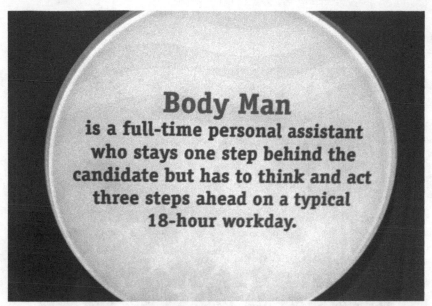

Photo of my job description explained in a gallery outside of the Des Moines, Iowa, NPR debate on December 4, 2007.

With then Senator Obama on our way to a campaign event in Las Vegas, Nevada, in March 2007.

The early days—with Richard Love, Richard Love Jr., Lynette Love, and me.

AAU Team Charlotte Royals (1996).

Duke football vs.
NC State (2003).

First career start for Duke against the Clemson Tigers in Cameron Indoor Stadium.

Duke basketball team meeting with George W. Bush.

Crammed in the campaign van en route to Coralville, Iowa, in December 2007.

During the early days of the campaign, when few had even heard the name "Barack Obama," most news coverage focused on Hillary Clinton and John McCain. I took the photo above on August 21, 2007, as the senator read a *New York Times* article about Clinton and McCain differing on Iraq.

The Harkin Steak Fry in Des Moines, Iowa, 2007. Obama for America out-organized the other campaigns with a huge show of support.

My perspective from most of the campaign rallies in 2007–2008. (*Above:* April 2008 rally in Greenville, South Carolina. *Below:* February 2008 rally in Fort Worth, Texas.)

soaps. She worshipped the Atlanta Braves. She could cook anything. Okra soup. Pistachio cakes. Gumbo.

She and her husband, John Wesley Jackson, began their married life in New Jersey, and raised my mother and her two brothers in Chicago. My grandfather loved my grandmother, but he also loved the bottle, and when he drank he became abusive. Soon enough Elise—"Leasee" to those beneath the Mason-Dixon Line—got fed up and decided making it on her own was less terrifying than dealing with her unpredictable spouse. She left her husband behind and moved south to be a single parent in Mount Pleasant.

She would go on to become the first African-American woman ever to work for the Social Security Office in Charleston. My grandmother was a tough, fearless advocate for African-Americans and for women, and she reared my mother to be the same. Elise believed in doing everything for herself. She saw dependence as a trap. She cut her own grass. She cooked all her meals from scratch. There was nothing she couldn't do, and she was *good* at everything. She was also kind and loving, leaving an open door to anyone. To me, she was Superwoman. Superwoman who could bake a pound cake that tasted like heaven. The bar she set was high.

I remember when I was a child, during one of my summers with her, she had this fake plant on her dining room table, and one afternoon I was playing with matches and the decoration caught on fire faster than hair dipped in kerosene. My grandmother didn't panic. She just rushed in, like, "I got this," extinguished the fire, then set her sights on me. All these years, she'd kept the table, burn mark and all. She simply bought another plant to cover it up and went on with her life.

My grandmother was eighty-three years old when she passed away. I rented a car and drove eleven hours from New Orleans to Mount Pleasant for the funeral. As I watched my mother break down, I too started to weep.

The trip forced me to consider my roots, the legacy I was inheriting. I came from a long line of strength. Family members who had sacrificed so much more than I ever would. How could I ever repay that debt?

I wondered too, would I be ready when my own parents passed away? Can you ever be ready?

My father, Richard, was one of nine children. There were more Love kids in his hometown of Valentine, Virginia, than there were traffic lights. My dad played high school basketball and wanted to play college, but that dream was out of reach. My grandparents didn't have the money or the time to travel. They were too busy working to provide for their family.

My father met my mother, Lynette, on the University of North Carolina Central campus. He spotted her and Leasee trying to get a massive trunk up to the fifth floor of the freshman dorm (no elevators) and offered to help them carry the load. Sparks flew. They were married before graduation.

My mother was the first in her family to attend college. My father was only the second in his, after his older sister. The opportunity was hard-won on both counts, and because of that, both of my parents recognized the value of an education and making the most of their time at school. They had witnessed what their family had done without so they could attend a university, something that was still very rare for African-Americans in those days. They expected the same conscientiousness and pride of place from me.

I can still hear my dad drumming in my ear, "Stand up straight. Look people in the eye. Speak up." My father was never a loud guy, but he had a strong physical presence. I remember when I was in grade school, when he left for work before sunrise, he would leave a belt on the doorknob of my bedroom as a reminder of what was waiting for me if I misbehaved at school.

Like me, my dad was a competitor. There wasn't much he loved more than winning. Basketball, cards, *Jeopardy*, pool, mowing the lawn. Whatever it was, he wanted to do it best. Including beating me in hoops.

We'd slug it out on our small, slanted driveway nestled in the rural neighborhood of Autumn Wood. Hot or cold, rain or shine, we played. Every bricked shot, the ball would roll down the hill into a creek, and I would gladly chase after it, so elated to be shooting baskets with my dad. It was without question a crappy court compared to Cameron Indoor Stadium or the other college and professional arenas I had a chance to play in, but it is also the court I miss the most.

There was no greater victory than beating my dad at home in a game of H-O-R-S-E. And just like the President, my father was fluent in trash talk. It didn't matter if it was a blowout or he won by one point; if he defeated you, he'd slyly let you and everyone in the house know about it, usually over the kitchen table or on the car ride to church. The message was always the same: I'm not that old yet. He would never let you forget it when he beat you at anything. No matter how old my father was, he kept competing, he never quit.

★ ★ ★

After my grandmother's service, there were still a couple of weeks left on combine training. But I decided not to return to the Big Easy. I stayed in North Carolina with my mom and dad.

I had been trained enough. I was ready to be home.

13

AT LEAST IT'S NOT FRIED WALLEYE

A big part of being a bodyman was making sure the candidate was fed. A hungry candidate (or President) was an underperforming one. During my time as personal aide on the campaign, I was responsible for planning a minimum of two meals a day, six days a week, in ten to twelve different cities. The challenge for any bodyman is finding the desired food at crazy hours, in far-flung locations, while the whole team is on the move.

Usually, I would start by emailing or calling someone on the ground. What was available? Where were the restaurants located? Were they open? How far were they from the event? Would the food be warm by the time the candidate was ready to eat? Then I'd select items off the menus. Often, I'd have to guess what the sure-to-be-starving candidate wanted to eat. That part was easy. Grilled fish.

Grilled chicken. As healthy as he could get on the road. He liked ranch dressing or vinaigrette. He liked sandwiches and fruit (Gala apples)—anything you could eat in a moving car or cramped airplane seat. If it dripped, forget it. If it started cold, all the better, because it was probably going to end up that way anyhow.

For the most part, the senator was relaxed about his meals. But there were days when he specifically wanted X. And Lord help me if he'd made his mind up about what he wanted and I delivered the wrong thing. Or if it came with mayo. Or was undercooked. Or soggy. If there was one thing you didn't want to watch, it was the time-pressed candidate scraping a gooey, loathed condiment off the only food he was going to eat for the next seven hours.

That happened a lot.

Sometimes he'd mutter, "This was the thirty minutes I had to myself, and now I can't even enjoy my meal."

All I could do was apologize. "I should have gotten this right." I understood. It wasn't about the food so much as that mealtime was his only reprieve from the stress of the day. He needed to refuel, physically and mentally. Especially during the primaries.

The strategy in Iowa was ninety counties in eighty-nine days. In Iowa, the caucus-goers have ideas. They feel their power, and they wield it like a *Game of Thrones* sword.

My memories of Iowa begin very fondly. I'd been there once before, in 1996, when I was fourteen and my AAU team, the Charlotte Royals, played in the 15 and Under National tournament at Drake University in Des Moines. I was there for a week, and at the time, it felt like a Hawaiian vacation. We ate a bunch of meals at the Old Country Buffet; we slept at the Embassy Suites. They had free breakfast! And HBO! And there was a casino nearby that my dad would go to after the games.

And then I went back for the primaries.

More than in any other state, the voters in Iowa have come to expect to be *engaged* (New Hampshire voters run a pretty close second). During the election season, they wanted to meet the candidate not once, but five times. They wanted him to come wash their car. They wanted him to phone their daughter and sing "Happy Birthday." They'd say, "Stop by for a barbecue and then maybe I'll give you my support." And then sometimes they wouldn't.

Obama gamely did almost everything the caucus-goers requested. For me, it was sometimes hard to watch. I appreciated that they had a very important role as the gatekeepers to American elections. But to my mind, it was always a bit weird that this selection happened in a state with an African-American population of around 2.9 percent. There were days on the campaign in Iowa when I used to joke with Marvin that I should stay in the car so I didn't cost us votes.

Don't get me wrong, the people in Iowa were nice. And the staff that we had on the ground there pulled together an amazing team. Paul Tewes, the state director, and Emily Parcels, the political director, assembled a motivated lineup of young people, mostly imports who came from all over the world to be field organizers for a cause and a movement.

They would knock on every door. "Are you registered to caucus? Who are you caucusing for? Do you know where you're going? Well, you should caucus for Obama." They were single-minded, flooding the neighborhoods, getting the word out.

We on the traveling team canvassed by plane. If we could land a plane someplace, we did. Mason City, Sioux City, Omaha (which is really Council Bluffs), Des Moines, Davenport, Cedar Rapids, Dubuque. We'd fly in, then get into a car and drive, stopping in every hamlet for events along the way—a town hall or maybe a sit-down meal. Then we'd get back on the road, drive another hour, and do another town hall, eat another meal. We'd do as many events in twenty-four hours as we could pack in, then find a Super 8 or a Merrick Inn and bunk with the entire staff until the next morning; then rise, rinse, and repeat.

The pace was inhumane. But it was what we needed to do to have any chance of getting a W. Along with a schedule that was bursting at the seams, there were the unique Iowa concessions. One in particular is seared into my mind like a cattle brand: the Maid-Rite Sandwich Shop.

As I mentioned, the candidate was particular about what he ate.

For the uninitiated, the Maid-Rite Sandwich Shop was famous in most rural parts of Iowa for its loose meat sandwich, a heap of coarsely boiled ground beef bigger than your average Chihuahua that is served spilling out of a platter-sized, fluffy white bun. With all due respect to the loose meat chefs, the sandwich is not what one would call a photogenic plate of food. I didn't order one myself, and I'll eat chicken wings and pork rinds from a gas station. The candidate, however, was aware that people in Iowa loved their loose meat sandwiches, and so down it went.

For months after, I would tease the senator with "Man, I cannot believe you ate that sandwich."

And he would smile and say, "Nobody can ever say I didn't want to win."

I'm pretty sure no other candidates were eating loose meat sandwiches. Senator Clinton probably didn't feel like she had to—everybody was predicting that she would be the nominee. At this point Obama was still very much the underdog, and feeling the pinch. For example, unlike what was rumored to be going on with other campaign staffs, there was a maximum salary on the Obama for America campaign of $150,000 for any employee, no matter how high-ranking. It was done for budget reasons. The Obama campaign had started from scratch. It depended on our people being young and hungry and motivated. Inside and outside the campaign, we were appealing to the heart. We sensed a shift coming, but we couldn't be certain. And then the Harkin Steak Fry happened on September 16, 2007.

The Harkin Steak Fry is held every primary season in Indianola, Iowa. The who's who of Iowa politics shows up, and the whole premise of the event is that it is a fundraiser for Senator Tom Harkin. But it is really a chance for the caucus-goers to check out the candidates in the middle of the primary race. Thousands of people pay $30 a ticket to come to Indianola, which is about an hour and a half south of Des Moines. The event is pretty much the Iowa State Fair of politics, with the candidates acting as the livestock vying for the blue ribbon.

The Obama Iowa team had organized a pre-rally outside the gates before the steak fry. Thousands of people turned up to back the candidate. Far more than most had even imagined would show. When you looked out over the crowd, all you could see was a sea of "Hope" signs and the soon-to-be iconic Obama "O." It looked like a red, white, and blue crop. The sight was astonishing. I remember thinking then, for the first time, *Barack Obama will win this state!*

The other politicians at the steak fry thought so too. It was a clear turning point in the race because no one had ever seen anything like it. All the other attendees were kind of surreptitiously peering over the fence, gobsmacked.

The senator waded through the giant crowd literally buoyed by a sea of support. Unlike any of the other politicians in attendance, who stood apart on a separate stage, Obama kept walking with the people, but he made his way through the entire throng. It was like a scene from *Rudy*. I bet he would have swallowed a thousand loose meat sandwiches to make that happen. Thankfully, he didn't have to. But his willingness and gameness struck me. If you want to realize your dream, it helps to have an iron stomach.

Which brings me to Amana, Iowa. A town of many fine qualities—organic, healthy dining options not among them.

A little history about Amana. It is one of seven towns that make up the Amana Colonies, a historical community formed by German immigrants who were escaping persecution in the 1800s. Those early homesteaders prided themselves on maintaining an almost completely self-sufficient local economy. So a hundred-plus years later, when the Obama campaign rolled into town, I looked at a menu of the one main local restaurant and surmised that they had been serving the same food since they founded the colonies. Find an animal, kill it, bread it, and fry it.

When the candidate and crew were departing Amana after the last event of the evening, preparing to head to another small town and another Motel 6, the candidate looked over to me and asked in a famished voiced, "So, Reggie, what's for dinner?"

When he asked the question, it quickly brought me back to the countless times when Coach K had grilled me during film sessions, his laser pointer following my image across the big screen, with everyone on the team watching along. "Reggie, what exactly are you thinking on this play?" he'd ask. It was technically a question, but a question with no right answer, and the moment it was sprung on me, I knew whatever I was about to say was going to be all kinds of wrong.

It was with that same sinking feeling washing over me that I responded to the candidate, "Sir, we have a choice between fried pork tenderloin sandwich and fried walleye."

I explained that the fried fish was the local favorite, and people from all the surrounding colonies came to this restaurant for the fried walleye. He ate the walleye. Unhappily. But its relative awfulness became a reference point for the rest of campaign. Anytime I delivered him a dubious meal, he'd say, "At least it's not fried walleye."

Like the day in the suburbs of Detroit when the only thing I could find was a Wendy's chicken sandwich, extra mayo. It was better than the walleye, but it didn't keep the candidate from giving me his take on fast food and how not only should he not be eating it, but neither should I.

"That stuff will kill you," he lectured.

"Even the McNuggets?"

"Reggie. You won't be young forever."

The fast-food debate lasted throughout the whole campaign (and into the presidency, during which Marvin and I insisted on eating at McDonald's in every foreign country we visited). Like our early morning workouts, the running argument about food seemed trivial on the surface, but it, too, provided building blocks in our boss-employee relationship. Lots of people were responsible for various critical aspects of Obama's campaign, but food is a nonnegotiable need. Without fuel, the engine stops running. Food can also be a comfort. Which, in the midst of a punishing campaign, can be hard to come by and as vital as anything else. This was never made more clear than after a long day in Los Angeles and Seattle.

It was December 2007. We'd had an especially long and difficult two days in Los Angeles, during which we were perpetually running late. On the second day, right before a Latino luncheon, Robert Gibbs started yelling at me about time management: "Why the hell is he late?"

As I tried to explain, the candidate came up and added his two cents, complaining that the schedule was jacked up and that he shouldn't be put in that situation.

So I tried to fix the lineup—moving calls to the car, shortening other events—because *I* didn't want to be the reason the candidate was an hour overdue at every other scheduled event that day.

The Latino leaders lunch was set for fifteen minutes, but given that we were already more than twenty minutes behind, it was looking more and more like a train wreck in the making. I warned the candidate, "Look, you can't stay here for more than twenty minutes, because we have a long day ahead and the schedule is very tight."

He just shrugged at me and said, "We'll shave time off the fundraiser."

That didn't happen.

The Latino event ran almost an hour. And the fundraiser went overtime. Which meant the candidate was beyond tardy for the conference call with African-American CEOs. To add lightning to the storm, after twelve minutes of trying, I couldn't get the phone to connect, so the CEOs were literally left hanging, and it was then that Obama turned to me and said through tight teeth, "Reggie, this is messed up."

And I, cracking from the day and the stress and the hours still left to go, stupidly replied, "Well, if you didn't stay so long at the luncheon, we wouldn't have this problem."

The air went still. It was like that eerie calm before a tornado swoops in and levels your entire house. Nobody said anything.

"Marvin," Obama finally said. "Talk to Reggie because I am not having this conversation with him."

So Marvin schooled me. After he had finished showing me the error of my ways, the other shoe dropped, and it was a jackboot. The candidate asked for his lunch.

"You got my taquitos, Reggie?" he inquired wearily.

Taquitos had been served up at the Latino leaders luncheon. Obama, of course, had either been working the room, giving a talk, or fielding questions, which never left him time to grab a bite to eat. I knew the bag of taquitos I'd been handed hours ago had long since gotten cold, so I hadn't bothered to bring it when we headed to catch the plane to Seattle.

"I left the taquitos at the venue, sir," I confessed. "I assumed you wouldn't want them; they were three hours old."

Obama looked at me with blank disbelief. I might as well have left his bag in the car again. I apologized, but the pin had been pulled on the grenade. We were way behind schedule; he was tired and hungry. And once again, I had failed at my job.

By the time the plane landed in Seattle, Marvin had made his best suggestion of the campaign: find the finest taquitos in the state of Washington. Admittedly, Seattle isn't as well known for its Mexican food as LA, but I found an adequate Mexican restaurant and got every type of taquitos they made.

Later that night, we drove to the last of three evening events, a forty-five-minute trip. I was sitting in the back of the Suburban, with the senator in the middle captain's chair, and Marvin up front in the passenger seat. When the senator asked what we had to eat, I started going through the usual list.

"We have some grilled chicken, we have grilled salmon . . ."

He interrupted me, shook his head, and said with obvious disappointment, "The same stuff?"

Then, as Marvin held up a large bag, I replied, "And, we have some . . . taquitos!"

He looked like he'd won the lottery. We all started laughing hysterically. Anyone looking in through the window would have presumed we were crazy. We probably were.

I earned some respect that day and I grew a bit on two counts. First, accountability: you make a mistake, you own it, and you do what you can to correct it—no matter how trifling the mistake may seem. I did just that. And the senator respected the move. Second, and perhaps more important: no matter how bad things felt, we all knew they could be worse. So if it was in our power to make them a bit better, we did. I made a habit of focusing on the silver lining. A crappy hotel gym was better than no gym. A delayed meal was better than no meal. And a mistake that yields a lesson is an opportunity.

As Obama enjoyed his taquitos dinner, all was forgiven. I knew it hadn't been the best twenty-four hours. But it hadn't been the worst either. I'd been in tougher situations before. And I had survived. As I would have occasion to say numerous times on the campaign trail: at least it wasn't fried walleye.

14

LET THE BEAR OUT OF THE CAGE

Politics is a dance to a song that never ends. Those who excel at what is truly a blood sport are those who eat, sleep, and breathe the beast. A campaign necessitates an almost pathological single-mindedness from all its participants—everyone from personal aide all the way up the chain of command to communication director to trip director to campaign manager, to the candidate. As Obama himself said, "In politics there may be second acts, but there is no second place."

If you sign on, you are signing up for eighteen-hour days. Forget weekends, Thanksgiving and Christmas and New Year's. Forget, too, your mental health, your diet, and your romantic relationships. Oh, and check your pride at the door. The time commitment is so punishing and abnormal that it makes NFL training camp look like an Easter egg hunt.

At any moment you might find yourself looking in the mirror and asking WTF you are doing with your life. Pressures weigh most acutely on the candidate. Which is why, sometimes, you need to let the bear out of the cage.

★ ★ ★

Late in February of 2008, we were traveling from Houston, Texas, to Brownsville. It was a day when the candidate was sapped. When that happened, Alyssa Mastromonaco's scheduling team decided to implement something called "BO time," a little window on the schedule where the senator could collect himself. A ten-minute reprieve from jumping on phone calls or giving interviews after a big rally or town hall. Sometimes there were unforeseen delays, events that ran long, or an emergency event that could only be handled by the candidate, but Marvin and I always tried like hell to protect BO time.

As we drove through Brownsville after a particularly fiery speech, the candidate overheard Marvin talking about a local celebration called the Sombrero Festival.

"Pull the car over," Obama directed.

"Sir, we aren't scheduled for a stop with Secret Service—" Marvin tried, but he was interrupted by the candidate.

"Pull over," the senator repeated. "I want to check out the Sombrero Festival. They've probably got some great food there."

Secret Service pulled over. And before we could count to ten, the candidate was out of the vehicle and absorbed into a massive crowd of people. He waded through the hordes, stopping at food booths, ogling the piñatas and sombreros, and giving the Secret Service multiple coronaries as he did.

Marvin just looked at me, shrugged, and said, "The bear is out of the cage. Somebody go get the tranquilizer gun."

The way I saw it, Obama not only needed a dose of freedom, he wanted to concretely reiterate that *he* was running the show. He wanted all of us to know that he was not a puppet. Not for the campaign. And not for anyone who thought they could wrangle him to do their bidding.

After the Sombrero Fest excursion, whenever Obama wanted to make an "off the record stop" (OTR) Marvin and I would promptly say in unison, "The bear is loose."

This happened early in the presidency, on his first international trip, to Ottawa, Canada, when Marvin made the mistake of suggesting a regional pastry treat called a Beaver Tail.

"Let's get one!" Obama said. And again, we were off to the races, the President unleashed, mobbed by the public like a rock star.

The Secret Service was so tweaked about the Beaver Tail stop that when we got back to the White House the next day, they sat down Marvin, the scheduling team, and me, and said, "If we ever do that again, there will be some real problems. And none of us will have jobs."

With the senator, there were always internal conversations and strife about doing public versus private events; how he was meant to interface with a city, state, or country that he was visiting for the first time.

Everyone had his or her own thoughts on what the strategy should be. The schedule was an iron triangle, the three sides consisting of mental health, physical health, and campaigning. There were only twenty-four hours in a day. How much of each of the three could you squeeze in? All the players, from Axelrod to family to press to staff to anyone with advice to give, encouraged or not, wanted their piece of the hourly pie.

For me, the most important thing was making sure the candidate got some rest. To be clear, no one was rested. The trick was not to push too far into exhaustion. Without a bare minimum of sleep came the slips of the tongue. The mistakes. Interviews were not going to be as effective if he wasn't sleeping at least a few hours. The aim was for five a night.

During the campaign, there was this big debate about whether or not to have a phone put on the aircraft. Eventually the phone arrived, but the senator didn't like using it. The connection was bad. And ultimately, midair calls were of such low quality they weren't worth making. Never mind that after seven events in one day, he didn't want to experience that frustration during the only free hour he had.

Juliana Smoot, our sweet-but-tough finance director from North Carolina, would ask, "How many calls did you make from the plane today?" (The phone had been her idea. A way to keep fundraising every spare second.)

I'd answer, "We tried, we really did."

Smoot was no dummy. She sensed our duplicity. The thing was, to stay sane, we all had to grab any break available. Like I did during a particularly grueling stint on the campaign trail in the winter of 2007 when I became the bear who needed to break out of the cage.

We were in Seattle, and all of us were feeling beaten up and frayed. It struck me like a lightning bolt that a trip to the tattoo parlor would be just the ticket to turn the momentum. (I'm no statistician, but I'd venture a large majority of the decisions to get a tattoo are made with a similar lack of foresight.)

So I made certain the senator had everything he needed for the night, then found Marvin and announced, "I'm going to get a tattoo."

"You're what?" He blinked, taken aback.

"I'm getting inked. I found this place called Under the Needle, and I'm going. You in?"

"One hundred percent." Which I didn't then and still don't think was true. I think he came along out of some parental instinct. Perhaps he had visions of my return looking like Mike Tyson, with an eye and neck tattoo or some sort of infection that would have left him responsible for doing my job. Regardless, I was grateful for the company.

We left the Westin Hotel at 1 A.M., grabbed a taxi, and arrived at the tattoo parlor to find the door locked. The sign read "Open," so I knocked on the door repeatedly.

After a few minutes, a grunged-out guy emerged from the alley hoisting a giant ladder and said, "Yo! Cut it out."

I explained I wanted to get a tattoo, that, yes, we knew what time it was, but that given our schedules 1 A.M. was the only free time we had.

The guy replied, slightly out of breath, "I'm D.Z. This is my place." Then he explained to Marvin and me that he'd locked himself out of his shop and that the ladder that was propped against the building on a Seattle-like incline—which was clearly three feet short of the second-floor window—was his way back in.

Not exactly confidence-building. But we pressed on, helping him break into his own joint, climbing two stories up into an open window that the ladder barely reached. It was like Super Mario Bros., tattoo edition.

Not long after we busted in, I got my first tattoos. I went with: "My Word, My Bond," on the inside of my right arm. And "My Boyz, My Blood," in the same spot on my left.

I chose those words to remind me of my focus and the value of friendship. Trust is everything to me. Loyalty is a close second. I knew I would never have to look far to find my center.

★　★　★

Three hours later, Marvin and I were back at work. He'd apparently shared with the senator what I'd done at Under the Needle.

"I heard you got a tattoo last night," Obama said.

I said, "Yes, yes, I did."

He shook his head very parentally. "Your mom isn't going to be happy with me. This happened on my watch."

I shrugged, not sure what to say.

A few days later, at a small holiday gathering in Des Moines, Mrs. Obama said to me in a motherly tone, "Barack told me you got tattoos."

I told her, yes, I had, and that I was really happy with them.

"Well, I'm happy they are in places you can't easily see," she replied, then added, "Just promise me you won't get any more."

I kept that promise until after the 2008 election. Marvin had just turned thirty-nine, and for his birthday during a presidential visit to Seattle, I came up with the great idea of the two of us going back to D.Z.'s shop.

This time we both got tattooed with 365, the number of electoral votes Obama had won. (In April of 2014, we did the same thing again, inking 332.)

I marked myself with my history. And with the history of this country. Like my word and my bond, these, too, would be with me forever.

15

ANGER MANAGEMENT

For much of my young adult life, I struggled with the fear that I was a cliché, seen by my peers as the black guy who acted white. Racism exists not only between races, but within races. And I wrestled with both sorts, wanting nothing so much as to be appreciated for who I was, not who either demographic expected me to be.

Everyone, no matter what age or class, craves acceptance. And people are typically drawn to things and to people that are similar and familiar to themselves. This dynamic makes it hard for us to stretch or reach for things that don't gracefully fit into our typical cultural box.

In high school, I was one of the only black kids on my AAU team who didn't go to public high school. So the guys I played ball with always gave me grief. I also often felt like an outsider among the other students at my private school. Not only because I was of a different race, but because what was familiar to me at that point in my life was so different from their experiences.

In truth, I didn't belong anywhere. I was a party of one. Or at least that's how I felt when I was a young black man stumbling toward adulthood in the Deep South. At Providence Day I was surrounded predominantly by affluent Caucasian kids. Closer to home, my friends played for their public school teams, which were comprised overwhelmingly, if not entirely, of African-Americans. The difference was stark and obvious, and it seemed like the only people comfortable talking about it were my friends, who used the fact to needle me whenever we played.

★ ★ ★

It was three days after the Black & Brown Forum and the Heartland Forum when we attended the NPR debate in Des Moines. And it was there, on December 1, 2007, that I managed to ruffle the feathers of not only a caucus-goer, but also several members of my own crew, including the candidate.

The debate was held in the Historical Building of Iowa, inside of which was an exhibit explaining the history and the process of the Iowa Caucus. I took the tour, and as I walked through the whole thing, I noticed that there weren't any black people depicted in the entire exhibit. There was possibly one mixed-race, handicapped, Republican veteran. But that was it as far as a depiction of the black caucus-goer went.

I wasn't *trying* to make trouble with the curator, but I couldn't keep myself from commenting on the obvious racial inequity. When I asked where the black folks were, the curator stiffened. She argued that there were plenty of African-Americans in the exhibit. Which there were not. Unless you included brown people—two Asians and one Native American.

Again, I wasn't trying to be a jerk. But the reality was, if you are going to go through the trouble of staging a display of one of the most critical parts of our American democracy, you might want to include *all* Americans, no?

Marvin pulled me aside and said, basically, "Zip it." I was, in his mind, making trouble.

"Trouble finds me," I answered, half-joking and somewhat incredulous that nobody seemed to be bothered by the glaring omission of a significant part of the population, which happened to include the candidate. "Marvin, you're crazy if you think it's wrong for me to mention the fact that there are no black people in an exhibit that's supposed to showcase the process of selecting the President of the United States."

"And *you* are crazy," he shot back, "if you can't see how your attitude is damaging."

"You've got to be joking."

"Enough, Reggie."

It was a good old-fashioned standoff. Later, I asked other staff members what they thought, and everyone sided with Marvin. Even the candidate, who explained, "Coming off as an angry black man turns caucus-goers away from Barack Obama."

I went quiet, but I was thinking, You *think this is angry? You haven't seen me angry.*

But I knew they were right.

I later watched the senator learn firsthand how little leeway there is when it comes to sharp, blunt truths. At an April 2008 fundraiser in San Francisco the candidate made an honest but not well-received remark about how when working class voters are beset by economic hardship in their towns, "they get bitter, they cling to guns or religion or antipathy toward people who aren't like them."

True as it was, there was immediate backlash, with the opposition leading the charge that Obama's comments were evidence of his "elitism." The comment was picked up by all the national media and even trickled down into many critical local media markets in swing states.

The candidate quickly apologized and explained the context of the comment, and after that, he continued to craft and hone his messaging because often the message you want to communicate isn't the message that is received. I remember looking at juxtaposed *New York Times* and *Wall Street Journal* front page stories that came to opposite conclusions. Essentially one story said, "Obama too tough on . . . X," and the other said, "Mr. Obama weak on . . . X." The candidate often found himself in a double bind, damned if he spoke, damned if he didn't. I felt like this standard was not applied to other candidates or members of Congress, where tantrums, red-faced rages, and even crying were viewed as evidence of passion, commitment, and strength.

In some ways Iowa, and the whole progression that followed into the White House, was a kind of time warp, with Obama needing to take every high road ever built, to be the Jackie Robinson of politics—calm, cool, and in control no matter what was flung his way.

He got flack from both sides. There were, of course, your garden-variety racists throughout the campaign season who would wave their middle fingers and hateful signs as the motorcade rolled through their neighborhoods. I particularly remember signs with letters painted in red reading, "Obama is a Muslim." Crazy stuff. There was passive stereotyping, too. For example, the people who always assumed I was the security guy. He's tall. He's black. He *must* be security, and he's probably a basketball player.

When they would address me with that assumption, I always responded with some variation of "No, you want the old, white, Clint Eastwood–looking dude over there."

Then there were constituents in the African-American community who seemed to feel that in the same way issues were targeted toward women and LGBT populations, similar considerations and nods should come to them from a black candidate. There was an inordinate amount of pressure to be the first African-American president. The senator was carrying the hopes and dreams of generations in a way no other candidate had. But Obama took care to explain that he couldn't just be "a president for black people." That wasn't just bad politics, it was a bad strategy, if he intended to make civic change. If you improve national education and health care, foster a sustainable economy, and help create jobs, it will lift everybody up. These fundamental building blocks help all people live the American dream.

At the end of the day, the candidate had a job to do. He couldn't engage in a verbal back-and-forth with every angry critic who said something absurd to the press about him. As a candidate, if he ever let it get personal, it only affected the wider campaign. And once he became president, an emotional display just hindered his ability to get future business done. So he sucked it up.

Not that Obama didn't allow himself to vent a little steam, often at the White House Correspondents' Dinners, where he used humor to shine a light on the silliness of agitators like Ted Nugent, Sheldon Adelson, or Donald Trump and his birther movement.

One of my favorite moments was when he said in his usual deadpan voice during the 2011 dinner, "Tonight, for the first time, I am releasing my official birth video." And then we screened the opening scene from *The Lion King*.

He followed it up with another great zinger. "I just want to make clear to the FOX News table that that was a joke. That was not my real birth video. That was a children's cartoon. Call Disney if you don't believe me. They have the original long-form version."

But the dinner only came once a year. The rest of the time, Obama often made a conscious decision not to let anger define him, no matter how justified it might have been. Like when South Carolina representative Joe Wilson screamed, "You lie!" in the middle of a State of the Union Address. Obama's factual statement that proposed health care legislation wouldn't provide free health coverage for illegal immigrants had inspired Wilson's gross breach of decorum.

The President calmly looked at a flushed, sweaty Wilson and responded, "That's not true." Every day, in all ways, he was forced to live above the fray. His behavior then and always was invariably presidential, carrying in public the dignity of his office just as presidents before him had done. Except, of course, it couldn't be left at that. Because of race. And our country's complicated relationship with it. He was never just a senator, or just a candidate, or just America's forty-fourth president.

★ ★ ★

The model-minority mandate was not exactly exotic in my world. My mom and dad had always stressed to me that when you allow yourself to get visibly angry, all you're doing is giving your opponent the upper hand. "Rise above it," they'd tell me.

This was easier said than done, especially during my junior year of high school.

I'd been at odds with my high school basketball coach. We had one kid on our team who was a great shooter. But that was the extent of his talent. Still, he played. And he was often praised and rarely criticized.

It felt to me that I wasn't coached the same and my coach was the hardest on me. It felt race-based, because it felt like I was constantly being singled out even though I would often lead the team in scoring and rebounding and defend the opposing team's best player. After three seasons of playing for my high school, I decided I wanted to transfer to another school, where there would be more students who looked like me.

But it was too late. My parents had already paid the tuition for the coming year. And they wouldn't hear about a transfer anyway. I had been admitted to the best academic high school. And I was going to graduate from there.

Furious, I lodged a protest. Every single day, I wore the same exact black hoodie. I grew my hair out. I would attend the prep school. But I was not going to be turned preppy.

By the winter, I looked like a hobo. My hair was unkempt and ratty. My hoodie was tattered and smelled like a bus station. My dad would look me over every day and say nonchalantly, but clearly, "Son, you look like shit."

I knew he was right. But I didn't care. The protest was my way of controlling *something*. I was on an island at my high school, and I'd been mocked by my friends and teammates, who said that my school only played against a bunch of suburban rich kids, by which they just meant white. Even at sixteen, I was very well versed in how knotty and convoluted race could be. And I knew that if I acted on the outside how I felt on the inside, I would be consumed by anger and rage.

My father was right, there was only one choice. Turning that anger inside was only damaging myself. (Not to mention my dating life.)

After the end of basketball season, I cut my hair. I threw out that grubby hoodie. I did me the best way I knew how. I stood tall.

★ ★ ★

Being a part of the Obama team revealed so much to me about race in America. I honestly believe that most people are good human beings.

We share the same ambitions and desires to have opportunity, to raise a family, to retire with dignity. We are a big country, and we are diverse, but we aren't often pushed out of our comfort zones. If you live in a neighborhood with no black people, it's easy to believe a stereotype is real. It can take a while to form one's own independent opinion. But it can happen. I've seen it myself, repeatedly, when I've traveled to tiny towns and conservative enclaves and observed as Obama won over the hearts and minds of citizens who before would have been afraid to open their doors to a black man.

I believe the world is improving. Globally, things are getting better, more transparent. There is better advocacy for races, genders, and sexual orientations now. More frankness across demographics. I can't help but be optimistic. I have it so much better than my parents did, and they so much better than my grandparents. The path is nothing but up. It is hard for me to complain.

Of course there are still inequalities. No one being honest with him- or herself can survey the country, or for that matter the world, and not admit that. But the way I look at inequality is that I should spend my time taking advantage of the opportunities I do have, rather than griping about the opportunities I don't. Life will never be evenly balanced. You hope and pray for parity. When you can, you work toward it, you even fight for it. But more than anything, you just want a chance. When one is given to you, you recognize it and make the most of it, and if you're honest you'll admit that you have just incurred a small debt. That, hopefully, is paid off down the line to someone coming up behind you. Mentor. Volunteer. Put yourself out for a cause greater than yourself. Make a difference.

The President often told me that the best way anyone can make a difference is by making his or her voice heard. At minimum, vote. Better yet, participate in the process. Educate yourself and, when it makes sense to do so, educate others. He showed me you can't allow yourself to be discouraged by the political process or by the prevailing attitudes of the country, explaining, "The things that discourage you are the very reasons you *should* become involved and participate in the political process."

During the campaign, we'd be at events long past time because the candidate wanted to respond to every question. He believed in hearing all the voices in the room, not just his own. He welcomed differences of opinion. He saw the value in listening to every side. It was a different sort of leadership than I'd been exposed to before. Obama understood that challenge and confrontation could lead to, if not resolution, then understanding. He felt that any conversation was better than silence. Engagement, not stomping off the court in anger, he showed me, was how the ball got carried forward. And even though America has its problems, Americans have an incredible capacity to grow. Individuals evolve, and with them society. Change is the rule, not the exception.

I know how easy it can be to get caught up in the here and now. But every moment—whether it is a bad free throw, a failed exam, or just an idiotic mistake—is just that: a snapshot. Not the whole game of your life, or of our culture. I understand caring about the score *right now*, about who won a given championship, or election. But seasons are long and so are careers, relationships, and lifetimes. Don't be afraid to pass the ball.

16

SUNLIGHT IS THE STRONGEST DISINFECTANT

*As Barack Obama's confidence in me developed and eased into a profes-*sional reliance, so did my investment, not only in the job, but also in the larger dream of the candidate's election to the presidency. Hearing the senator speak, seeing how his brain worked, watching his commitment to improving the lives of Americans deepen day after day—all of that fortified my loyalty. He would tell me, "If I'm in Washington and I can't do the right thing for the American people, then I don't want to be there. I'd rather vote the way I believe, even if it costs me the ability to get reelected."

This conviction is why he spoke out against the Iraq War well before it was popular to do so. And why he was against the Patriot Act. And why he responded so swiftly and effectively to the BP Deepwater Horizon oil spill. Obama wasn't responsible for the lax regulations that allowed that environmental calamity to happen. But, as he explained to me, "I don't have the luxury of saying this isn't my problem. Ultimately, everything sits on my plate. And I can't pass it to someone else."

He showed me that no matter how insurmountable a catastrophe appears to be, you never throw your hands up and say, "I'm not handling this one." It was a tenacity I had seen in the sports world, when my team was down twenty points or in the midst of a humiliating season, and we had no choice but to rally and trudge on. But until working for Obama, I'd rarely seen that depth of persistence and drive in the wider world, and I had never seen what a force for change it can be when matched by an ability to see a problem through to a solution.

This doggedness was even more impressive because I saw how few people seemed to notice it outside of the campaign or the White House. I recall having dinner with a friend's mother one night after Obama took office, and she was complaining that the President hadn't done anything for education. This statement blew me away. As I'd learned to do from my boss, I calmly began to temper her ill-informed belief with facts. I ticked off the policies I knew of firsthand, told her of the President's confabs with the teachers' unions, reminded her of the educator pay raises, the implementation of Race to the Top, and a whole host of other improvements the President had initiated. I agreed that none were perfect solutions, but they were *solutions*, and more to the point, they were steps that would steer our country in the direction of solving problems that had divided citizens culturally and economically, and limited their access to education and opportunity.

As time passed, I had to get used to the gap, sometimes vast, between what the public perceived was happening in D.C. and what was actually getting done in the White House. The President taught me the value of transparent government, honesty, and hard work. He also taught me the importance of navigating by your core principles rather than by public perceptions. In D.C., everyone is always keeping score. Which makes it hard to move forward. There are twenty-year-old grudges. Many politicians don't seem to get the concept of "next play." Obama was different.

On the Democratic side, there were some who complained that Obama was no Bill Clinton. Even after I was out of the White House, reporters would email and call me. They'd argue that Obama was aloof and was an atypical president and politician because he had a different appetite for entertaining than President Clinton did. Sometimes supporters also complained about access to the administration. In some ways, the grousing was earned. This administration was tough on quid pro quo. Obama *wasn't* doing business as usual; there was actual change in his administration.

I found it ironic that Obama was criticized for not wanting to hang out with Speaker John Boehner because he preferred to have dinner with his daughters and his wife. I also found it problematic that people were judging his performance and making comparisons across generational lines. What a president with two young children does after work varies greatly from what a president with adult children does. Or questioning his leadership of the party without factoring in how the Democrats are split across several different issues—LGBT, immigration, women's rights, to name just a few—whereas the Republicans, at least in their loathing of Obama, are steadfastly homogenous. The line he needed to walk was always much narrower.

If it was maddening for me, I could only imagine how wearisome it must have been for the President. Casting aspersions often seemed the default mode of Washington politics, and shadows of doubt were often good enough to grind progress to a halt. But Obama was used to the shade throwing and believed that the best cure for shade was sunlight. Something he proved time and again during the campaign, never more so than when he was getting blowback from his association with his former pastor, the Reverend Jeremiah Wright.

Wright had caught national attention in 2008 when fragments of some ill-advised sermons he'd made years ago were unearthed and made public. Obama emphatically denounced the statements in question, but critics would not let it go. His instinct was to address the controversy head-on.

"I'm not sure this is such a great play," Axelrod warned, echoing the sentiments of the entire team, who didn't want the candidate to wade into the turbulent waters of racial politics in America. But the senator would not be swayed.

He was set to give a speech to about one hundred people in Philadelphia, but he tossed the original script and started over, completely rewriting the speech by hand. The result was titled "A More Perfect Union," and it read in part:

I have already condemned, in unequivocal terms, the statements of Reverend Wright that have caused such controversy. For some, nagging questions remain. Did I know him to be an occasionally fierce critic of American domestic and foreign policy? Of course. Did I ever hear him make remarks that could be considered controversial while I sat in church? Yes. Did I strongly disagree with many of his political views? Absolutely—just as I'm sure many of you have heard remarks from your pastors, priests, or rabbis with which you strongly disagreed. But the remarks that have caused this recent firestorm weren't simply controversial. They weren't simply a religious leader's effort to speak out against perceived injustice. Instead, they expressed a profoundly distorted view of this country—a view that sees white racism as endemic, and that elevates what is wrong with America above all that we know is right with America; a view that sees the conflicts in the Middle East as rooted primarily in the actions of stalwart allies like Israel, instead of emanating from the perverse and hateful ideologies of radical Islam. As such, Reverend Wright's comments were not only wrong but divisive—divisive at a time when we need unity; racially charged at a time when we need to come together to solve a set of monumental problems—two wars, a terrorist threat, a falling economy, a chronic health care crisis, and potentially devastating climate change; problems that are neither black or white or Latino or Asian, but rather problems that confront us all.

The speech resonated for the campaign and the country. The senator had gone against all conventional wisdom, as well as the wishes of most of his expert staff. He'd thought for himself. Acted. And tackled an issue that no one else would touch. He shined a light on a bigger picture.

I'd grown up in a church not unlike Wright's. I understood the layers beneath the issue and the touchiness on all sides. Obama's speech moved me. I'd read it on paper several times, but hearing the words delivered in his powerful, heartfelt voice was a revelation. And not just to me. It essentially killed the controversy dead for the remainder of the campaign and reminded our nation that race relations were being inadequately addressed.

In that one hour, the senator taught me the value of not sweeping problems under the rug. That only by addressing issues openly and directly can one eventually move on and grow from them. Did he convince everyone? Of course not. You never will. But reasonable people are open to hearing a case well made, and it is reasonable people who get most of what must get done done. Obama spoke to them, and they listened.

When the speech was over, I passed the senator the handwritten pages he'd penned the night before. "One for the history books," I said, optimistic and proud of my boss in a brand-new way.

17

USE YOUR VOICE

It isn't possible to estimate how many meetings, fundraisers, and rallies we attended throughout the campaign, but I do know that one of the most meaningful experiences on the trail was also one of the tiniest.

Early on in South Carolina, the senator met with a state representative in Columbia, and asked for her vote. She said she would consider supporting the candidate if he would agree to visit her hometown of Greenwood. A month later, we were back down south, driving several hours to Greenwood for the promised visit and Obama rally.

At first, we thought we'd parked at the wrong place. There was no one around. When we entered the building, our impression didn't change. It was a ghost town. Dark, quiet, and the opposite of confidence-building. After further inspection, we stumbled upon our potential supporters. All ten of them.

As the senator sucked it up, swallowed his understandable disappointment, and began to work the room, we heard a jarring shout from the corner.

"Fired up!"

We all swiveled our heads simultaneously like prairie dogs, checking out the source of the startling racket. It was a petite, older woman in a large church hat.

"Fired up!" she shouted again into the largely vacant room.

And without any prompting, the nine other folks gathered at the field house chanted back: "Ready to go!"

The little old lady yelled again, with more conviction, "Fired up!"

"Ready to go!" the small crowd yelled back.

And so it went. At first, we were confused. Nothing like this had ever happened on the trail before. But there was no resisting the energy in the room. The cheering was infectious. By her sixth cry of "Fired up!" every member of our team joined in, "Ready to go!"

What had started as a dismal hour we couldn't wait to get through turned into the most lasting rallying cry of the campaign. We later learned that the woman who started the chant was a city council member named Edith Childs, who also moonlighted as a private investigator. She was known around town for leading the same back-and-forth at all the rallies and parades. And by the time we left Greenwood, we were, in fact, "Fired up and ready to go!"

For the rest of the election season, whenever we were seized with lethargy or dragging our heels, the senator would say, "Fired up!" And the rest of us would holler back, "Ready to go!" It never failed to lift our spirits, and it was a deep comfort to hear little Edith Childs's voice in our heads, pushing us on.

★ ★ ★

The more time we spent in each other's company, the more I marveled at Obama's naturally inquisitive nature—often the significance of a question from him wouldn't become apparent to me until days or weeks later. He had an insatiable appetite for information. I would get emails at 3 A.M., questions he wanted me to follow up on. The man never took a day off. No detail was too small for him. He was never afraid of looking like he didn't have the answer, but he worked tirelessly to try to understand all sides of a position. I saw how much more strength and authority his curiosity gave him. Far better than the bluster and pride of trying to be omniscient all the time.

More to the point, once he dove in with the questions, you knew you needed to have a deep understanding of the subject, and if you couldn't explain why you thought a certain way or were suggesting a particular course of action, he would know. He would want to know not just content, but most importantly, your reasoning—why now, why not sooner, or why not later? He would expose ideas and solutions that hadn't been considered. There was no room for bullshitting or not thinking things through. There was no skating by on empty opinion. You learned in a hurry that if you were going to speak, you'd better know what the heck you were talking about.

Obama was also big on understanding the character of people. If he was talking with you, chances were he was asking questions.

"How old are your kids?" "What school are they in?" "What books are they reading?" "What time do they go to bed?"

And he listened to the answers. There was never a non-inquisitive moment. He would ask and lean forward to listen, and then he would ask something else. He was exceptional at making people feel at ease one-on-one, whether the person was royalty or a janitor. Obama never viewed himself as bigger than life or better than others. He knew that once the game is over, the king and the pawn go back into the same box. He also saw himself as a conduit for the American people, people like Edith Childs.

That stop in Greenwood, South Carolina, shifted my perspective in many ways. There are no small events; every play matters. You never know what will happen, and honoring your promises matters more than you can ever know.

Maybe you don't think you'll be able to make a difference, but everyone can be a leader in their own community. You can decide to be politically active. You can inspire with the smallest gesture. You can be fuel for a larger fire.

More than anything, that visit showed me the power of a single voice. And how if you open your mouth and use it, you can change the world.

18

PLAY IT OUT

I knew my life had taken a dramatic turn when the thing that made me happiest in the world wasn't an evening with a woman I was charmed by, or Duke winning a game, but spending two consecutive nights in the same hotel. During the campaign that particular luxury became my white whale, the pinnacle of pleasure.

I was not alone in my appreciation of staying put. Every time I told the senator that we wouldn't be packing up until the next day, he would visibly relax. "Now, that," he'd say, "is the best news of the day."

Can you imagine what it would be like to pack and unpack every single morning and night? Seriously. Every morning, pack a bag, and then get in late in the evening and unpack (or at least find your toothbrush and clothes for the next day), then repeat, often twice in the same twenty-four hours. It was the worst. But I can say with unquestionable authority, I'm now one of the foremost experts on luggage and packing. I sometimes feel like a walking advertisement for Tumi, Samsonite, and WallyBags. Still, like everything else on the job, it took me a while to figure it out. And it provided an early lesson in how significant the seemingly insignificant can be.

In the beginning, I used your standard duffels and garment bags. But average luggage wasn't really built for campaign travel, and time and again the candidate's clothes would wrinkle. More often than not one of the hangers grouped at the top of a garment bag would wriggle free and find its way to the bottom, dragging its suit and maybe a shirt with it. Unpack the bag and there they would be, rumpled. Suffice it to say, no one blames luggage for long. Eventually, they look to the guy lugging the luggage. Nor did anyone love it when a week's worth of clothing got damp from being left plane-side in the rain or snow.

My salvation came in the form of the WallyBag, which had a clip that kept all the hangers in one place. It was also durable and waterproof. I bought ten of them. Mrs. Obama used one. Marvin used one. I would give them as gifts to colleagues who often complained about the rigors of travel. I also got some waterproof duffels for gym clothes. I became the luggage whisperer. It only took me thirteen months. But once I did, it was a problem (an admittedly minor one) solved, freeing up time and energy for bigger hurdles.

That's what happens on a campaign (and later what happened in the White House)—you appreciate the small victories. We still aimed for the highlight reel–worthy successes, of course. But every day doesn't end or start with a slam dunk. Disappointment and setbacks are the rule. And particularly on a campaign, you grab your creature comforts when and where you can. So I found myself doing happy dances about things like luggage, warm cookies at check-in, or a twenty-four-hour McDonald's within walking distance of the hotel.

Having been cut from two NFL teams and my middle school basketball team back in seventh grade, I was used to unwanted no's and dreams deferred. As an athlete, you learn quickly that failure doesn't take away from the work, and that courage means pressing on no matter how many failures are in your wake. You *prepare* to win, and you always play to win, but sometimes even great preparation and playing doesn't yield a win. If you are in the game long enough, you see it all. The heartbreak. The miracles. The whims of fate. The soul-crushing upsets. David beating Goliath.

I remember the first buzzer beater I ever hit. It was during the state tournament in Mount Airy, North Carolina. I was fourteen years old, and Ken Perry, my coach at the time, said, "Look, if you guys just get us close, we can win."

Coach Perry was this old-school, grizzled African-American, really tall, walked with a limp. And we were the Bad News Bears of the tourney. Our jerseys were cheap, royal blue—for our team name, the Royals—with bright orange writing across the front.

Our opponent was King's Mountain, a remarkable, talent-filled team that seemed to win every year. They had these giant twins who were built like tanks. I think one of the kids' names actually *was* Tank. Even so, that Sunday we had the game of our lives. Just like coach wanted, we found ourselves super-close. Part of me didn't believe we could win. With time running down, we ran a play. It didn't work. And I found myself in the corner with the ball. I heaved it up, and holy crap, it went in! The buzzer sounded. Everyone flooded the court. It was mayhem. We'd won, even though the opposing team was far better—except for that Sunday afternoon.

That afternoon taught me the importance of playing it out. Sometimes you get lucky. Sometimes it is simply your day. Regardless of the odds, you play to the finish because that's what it means to compete. If outcomes were predetermined, playing the actual game would have no value.

At a later game of the fifteen-and-under nationals, in Des Moines, Iowa, we got beat by the Atlanta Celtics in the elite eight, where I missed a wide open three-pointer to tie the game up. We packed up our bags and left town having battled our hardest. The dream was dead for another season. I had no idea how familiar that feeling would be a short time in my future.

Presidential campaigns are a 24-7 ordeal. You go where the people are, period. There is no calling in sick. There are no snow days. As Robert Gibbs would say, "Once you're in, you're in."

I recall one scorcher in Iowa, it must have been 101 degrees outside, and we were all standing around sweating into our suits—Marvin, the senator, all of us trying not to look disgusting while the fabric clung to our wet skin like toilet paper to a shoe.

I turned to the candidate and said, "At least I'm not at training camp getting crushed by the likes of Flozell Adams and Larry Allen [guys who could bench press seven hundred pounds]. This is much more bearable, it's just hot."

He laughed, and we continued to talk about what a Bill Parcells training camp is actually like. I told him every practice was full speed and full contact, even if it was against NFL policy. Parcells believed in practicing in game conditions and at game speed, and who is going to argue with a guy with two Super Bowl rings?

After I'd finished my fourth year of football at Duke, I went to Green Bay as an undrafted free agent in a package deal with a few other players. I didn't make the roster, which wasn't a surprise, as the guys I was competing against were much better than me—Donald Driver, Robert Ferguson, Javon Walker—and I knew going in that I was a long shot. The following year I ended up at Dallas as an outside linebacker. Bill Parcells had called me and asked if I would come and play defense. The Tuna wanted me? I'm there!

I arrived April 2005. To play defense, I put on twenty-five pounds to get to 250, and learned yet another position. I felt sick most of the time, trying to keep the weight on while running around sweating it out in 110-degree heat. I was not built for that position, and eventually we all agreed on that point, and I was released in September.

Long story short: everyone can't play, but everyone can play it out. I think life is about windows of opportunity, and while sometimes they open for you, other times they don't. What football provided me with was a world class education at Duke, and it also taught me endurance and helped me to better understand what it meant to persevere. It taught me toughness. This came into play in the most unlikely of places: Iowa.

"I don't know how anybody does that stuff," Obama said when I described the practices to him.

"For some people they don't know any other option," I answered. "Besides, when you want something bad enough, you go after it."

He nodded. *That* he understood. And soon enough I came to see just how much. Obama was not a man who gave up on his dreams. Once in office, he got the budgets passed. He repealed "Don't Ask, Don't Tell." But he couldn't win them all. And when he was thwarted, he would say, "We didn't win today, but eventually this will right itself. It's inevitable."

Never did that feel more true than the night the Affordable Care Act passed. The President had believed in making the principles of the ACA a reality since before he was elected U.S. senator.

During the campaign, the candidate would always say how he wanted to be the type of president who "gets things done." He didn't want to be the type of leader who worried about reelection or the polls or what people thought he owed them. He wanted to do what was best for the American people.

I remember, shortly after I'd begun working as his personal aide, the first time the senator told me how he'd lost his mother to ovarian cancer. He said, "The reason health care is an important thing to me is because my mom passed away at fifty-two years old. She wasn't thinking about coming to terms with her own mortality. She had been diagnosed just as she was transitioning between jobs, and she wasn't sure whether insurance was going to cover the medical expenses, because they might consider this a preexisting condition." His voice filled with fresh agitation when he spoke about her passing. Health care was not a campaign "issue," but rather a mission sprung straight from his heart.

A couple of times on the road, he suddenly said, "We are going to get this done." Once he was president, even when people on our team intimated that the party should be focusing on other issues, he never flinched. Like the night of his debate with candidate Romney, when the governor was snarlingly labeling the ACA "Obamacare," and Obama calmly responded, "Go ahead, I like that, because I do care. *Obama* cares."

The night the ACA passed, the feeling I most remember is "whew." The votes went back and forth until the last minute and required a ton of political capital. Phil Schiliro and his legislative affairs team were working for votes up until the final seconds.

We had reason to believe the act was going to pass, but we were all still really nervous. It was a late night, and the President stayed in the residence until the vote officially commenced. Then he came down and joined the entire staff, which had now assembled in the Roosevelt Room to watch C-SPAN together.

The President still had folks on the floor whipping up votes, and we were tracking the progress, but we weren't ahead of the news. When the outcome was final, we shared the excitement and thrill and pride. He'd done it. Right at the buzzer. People thought it couldn't be passed; they bet against him. But he proved them wrong. Just as he had in the primaries. Just as he will no doubt continue to do over and over throughout his tenure in the White House.

If Obama had given credence to the noise he heard, not just about health care, but about the countless other thorny issues that popped up daily, he would have never achieved anything of lasting value. He would have been stuck in neutral, a tire spinning in mud.

To watch the journey that something as improbable as the ACA took from presumed fruitlessness to commonplace reality showed me that anything is possible if you put your back into it. The whole world can give you one message—about yourself, about your dreams, about your potential—and you can choose to politely tell the world that you aren't listening, that, in fact, you hear a different tune, and that you intend to dance to the music in your head, not theirs.

19

YOU CAN'T BUY MOMENTUM

I call it "mo."

Momentum. You can't order it from Amazon. You can't turn it on or off like a light switch. But sometimes, if you are lucky, you put yourself in a position to happen upon it. And when mo sweeps you up, you ride the wave and let it take you where it wants you to go.

Mo happened during the championship season at Duke my freshman year. Mo took over my AAU team when we won the state championship and beat King's Mountain at the buzzer. And, as the world witnessed in 2008, mo most definitely happened with the Obama for America campaign a few weeks after he was declared the official Democratic candidate. David Axelrod said it reminded him of Jordan going for 69 against the 1990 Cleveland Cavaliers.

Obama always had swag. Even when the campaign was hitting

rough patches, we still saw record turnouts and had folks fainting after a hug or a handshake. Supporters would hang off the sides of buildings, angling to get a glimpse of the candidate, which I was sure was going to end in tragedy, but, thank God, never did.

Sometimes people would burst into tears. They'd get on their phones and call everyone they knew. "It's Obama! It's Obama!" I cannot remember how many times I held my breath as someone hoisted up a baby and leaned dangerously over a line of strangers to make sure the candidate spied parent and child. We once stopped near the Golden Gate Bridge so the candidate could take in the view on a sunny day, and people literally abandoned their cars on the street to stop and take a photo with him. Everyone wanted a hug. That was a thing. Kids would hug his leg. Women would hug everywhere. And then there were the trinkets. People wanted to give him a lucky charm. Poker chips. Patches from their military service. Rosaries. Thimbles with sayings carved on them. Rocks from the beach. Hankies from their grandmothers. Obama kept them all. He stored these collected charms and trinkets in a bowl, and he would turn to them for silent encouragement on dark days. But once the mo merged with his innate swag, there was no stopping him.

I remember one flight to Cedar Rapids when the weather was causing wicked turbulence. As we were being tossed around, a superstitious mind might have thought: *This is not the most auspicious start to our rural rollout in Iowa.* Except, none of that mattered. The day fired on all cylinders. When we got back to the airport to fly to the next stop that evening, the senator told Gibbs he wanted to watch *Bullworth* and *The Candidate* on the flight home.

"I thought we were making calls on the plane," I interjected.

"Relax, Reggie," Obama playfully shot back. It was the first time he'd ever told me that.

Before the mo, things on the campaign were tough. People would tend to be a little on edge about mundane stuff like having to make calls during drive times when they just wanted to nap, or small mistakes in scheduling. If there was ever a sharp response back to me, the candidate always apologized if he felt he'd been unfair. I usually explained that I had heard worse. Between playing college football and basketball, I'd certainly heard tougher and more vivid descriptions/comparisons of myself and my family members from my coaches in their attempt to motivate. Besides, I knew Obama wasn't really pissed at me. He was upset by the beating he was weathering in the media and the presumptive halo Hillary Clinton was enjoying from the Democratic Party and the pundits. During one visit in November to the offices of the *New York Times*, a reporter asked the candidate, "Is the only reason you're in the race because you gave a really good convention speech?"

Obama didn't waste a second responding.

"That's like you asking Hillary if she's only running because she was married to Bill."

As I said, you position yourself to benefit from momentum, and that means working for it. Nothing is going to happen if you don't show up, and the odds of something good happening when you do is increased when you show up prepared. You don't manufacture mo, but you sure can earn it.

Obama is as competitive as any person I've met. I've seen him win pull-up contests at fundraisers. Tennis, bowling, darts, skeet shooting—he wanted to master everything. Later, when he prepared to throw the first pitch for the MLB all-star game, he practiced his technique in the Rose Garden, marking off the correct distance from a major-league pitching mound to home plate. If the staff ever needed the candidate to do something he loathed, all we had to say was, "Do you want to win this campaign or not?" Without fail, whatever the onerous task was, he'd step up to the plate and perform.

Toward the end of the campaign, the mo made things easier. The process became more systematic. The candidate was firing on all cylinders. Which made it easier for me to do the same. The more he got into his groove, the easier he was to read and understand. It was also a function of repetition. He trusted me now. And he realized he could count on me.

Of necessity, I eventually learned how be effective at my job. During the campaign we juggled photo lines, meet and greets, sit-down meetings, meal meetings, meetings over drinks, coffees, and interviews. Interviews could include print, television, and radio, which we would either do all together or in twenty different combos. Sometimes we did them in person, other times over the phone or via satellite. For most satellite interviews, the network would get a sat truck, and the candidate would sit in a chair in front of a camera and have a live communication feed with the interviewer, usually a local newscaster from a battleground state. Everyone wanted the candidate or an event to look a certain way. Campaign staff had opinions for "messaging purposes." Media had opinions mostly for self-interested purposes. Our colleagues and supporters in the local markets also had ideas of how they wanted the candidate to interact with their neighbors and friends. It was a constant push and pull. And, of course, Obama had an opinion, too.

In Iowa, the debate swirled around the use of podiums. No one liked them, particularly the Iowa team. They looked impersonal. But it was hard to tack on specialized remarks for a given appearance without a podium to put the notes on. Expecting the candidate to rapidly memorize an additional half hour of facts about a complicated issue like biofuel or GMOs was a big ask. And so it became my job to master the balancing act.

I would tell our local teams, "All right, if you want the candidate to do extraneous or specific remarks, they have to be this length, or we're pulling out the podium." (Rick Siger, our Iowa lead advance person, always kept the podium in the trunk of one of the cars.)

Otherwise, the plan was to revert back to the stump speech, which the candidate had crafted himself and by then committed to memory.

People didn't always listen to me, of course. Particularly not in Iowa, where the podium was seen as a vote killer because it put a barrier between the senator and the caucus-goer. It wasn't "warm." My pointing out that "warm" was a relative matter, what with it being wintertime in Iowa, didn't help.

To make sure the candidate didn't struggle over pronunciations, names, or fun facts about each town, we made sure he had a card with this information written on it, or perhaps the names of the locals he needed to acknowledge. Those cards were as contentious as the podium. Everyone possessed a theory about who he should or shouldn't mention and why. It was much ado about the tiniest details. But the candidate *liked* acknowledging the locals. As a former state senator, he understood how much the gesture of being acknowledged meant. The rest of the team, not so much. They hated the shout-outs because they ate up the opening moments of an event, when the majority of the media coverage occurred.

"Sir, the acknowledgments are not working," Axelrod told the candidate after one event.

Obama pushed back. "We need to recognize people in the local communities so that they feel empowered. Then they'll go out and support our message and become champions for us. Besides, it's the right thing to do."

Acknowledgments continued even though the powers that be wanted them dead. In my opinion, those personal call-outs motivated people on our behalf far more than a national press sound bite did. It made them feel like they were part of Obama's team, and as such, they wanted to do their best to secure his victory.

On the campaign, thousands of people were working insane hours for what amounted to peanuts in salaried wages. They were there for a cause bigger than themselves or their bank accounts.

Obama's passion created a culture people longed to be a part of. His belief made us able to believe. It wasn't phony. True enthusiasm and commitment cannot be faked. They cannot guarantee you the gift of momentum. Commitment, belief, and effort are the fuels that make mo explosive.

★ ★ ★

Soon enough, the town halls began to overflow. There would be seven hundred confirmed attendees, with a capacity for twenty-five hundred, and then six thousand voters would show up for an opportunity to hear Obama speak. Once we gained traction and the ball was rolling, the senator really harnessed that energy. He inspired the crowds, taking question after question, ignoring our signals to stop. I remember watching him work his magic at one of the later town halls and thinking, *We may actually pull this off*. It wasn't a thought I usually had—I preferred to keep my head down and plow ahead. But the message of hope and change was contagious, and I had been infected.

When Election Day finally arrived, I almost couldn't grasp the finality of the moment. We'd been running nonstop for almost two years. And just like that, it was going to end. There was no gradual slowdown, no easing out of the race.

We'd had three events the day before, and then we landed in Chicago at 1 A.M. The lease for the plane ended the next day, so I stayed behind to clean it out; it was filled with briefing books, changes of clothes, gifts, and loads of other trinkets. I checked into a hotel at 2:30 A.M. and set my alarm for 5 A.M. so I could meet Obama at his house for the last official day of the campaign. He went to vote as soon as the polls opened at 6 A.M., a powerful image for all Americans to see bright and early on what would be a historical Election Day. Then we flew to Indiana to do an event with union organizers, came back to Chicago, and of course, played basketball.

We ran up and down for a couple hours with the senator's Chicago friends and other supporters who'd flown in for Election Day.

Obama was always tough attacking the basket, and he possessed a dominant mid-range jump shot. Mostly, he craved a good run, and wanted to play with folks with a high basketball IQ, people who wouldn't end up hurting the candidate. In my opinion, Obama's most defining on-court quality was that he was a very unselfish teammate. He cared more about winning the game than maximizing his own points and shot attempts. And so it was with his politics as well.

After our Election Day game, as a part of a last get-out-the-vote effort, the candidate had to do radio interviews—something that most politicians hate to do. The disc jockeys made him crazy, but the message was important. He was reminding people to vote. We finished by three in the afternoon, and then because the results had not yet started trickling in, he went back home to wait until it was time to leave for the watch party.

Around 6 P.M. the candidate made his way over to the Grand Hyatt on Michigan Avenue. The whole evening was surreal. The temperature had been unseasonably warm—seventy degrees in November in Chicago. It was either El Niño–related or the city knew something special was happening. People had been out on the streets, soaking up the sun like it was a spring day, and the mood seemed almost too perfect. I'd felt anxious, the way I used to feel on game day in college. I remember lying down on my hotel bed after a quick shower and feeling half-asleep and half-awake, suspended between the two states, not sure which direction I wanted to go.

That twilight stasis eerily mirrored how I felt about the election. It became clear by 5:30 CT, with the call on Pennsylvania and Ohio, that we were going to win. Barack Obama was going to be the next president. I was overjoyed. But I had also decided that I was not going to go to the White House. Marvin had been trying to change my mind for weeks.

Working in the executive branch was never my dream. Who wants to work for "The Man"? I'm joking, but the sentiment was real. Being a government employee was never on my bucket list. My father had worked for the Social Security office since he was twenty-five years old, and I'd seen how the job's built-in compromises could chip away at a person. I didn't want to be a part of a bureaucracy and its inefficiency.

At the hotel, I told Marvin I was thrilled for him, but that I would be charting a new course on my own. He said I was nuts. Maybe I was, but I was tired of the travel and was already looking into law schools and had spent time studying for the LSAT while crisscrossing the country with Marvin and the candidate.

"Good luck with that," he answered with trademark sarcasm. "Can't you see how this is the best opportunity in the world?" he pressed, shaking his head.

I shrugged. "What's so great about it?"

"Well, you get to see the world. You get to be close to power. You have a front row seat watching the most critical decisions affecting our planet being made, you know, shit like that, Reggie." Marvin sighed. "Everybody wants to work in the White House, dumbass."

He wasn't wrong. But his pitch didn't make it more desirable for me. It was like my mother urging me to eat spinach and Brussels sprouts because they would make me faster and stronger. I could see the value. But I wasn't hungry for it.

The next day I took the afternoon off and met up with Darryl Scott and James Evans. They were friends from Duke who came in for Election Night and who didn't work on the campaign, and we sat on the roof of the Rock Bottom Restaurant, eating lunch and having beers. I was, for the first time in years, relaxed—finally a day without a to-do list.

"This is why I'm not going," I announced with some satisfaction. "This moment right now."

Three days later I was back with the president-elect on a flight to D.C. We were headed to a meeting with President Bush and the first lady. For weeks Obama had been ribbing me about my best friend, Chris Duhon, exiting Obama's beloved Bulls, talking trash about how Chris, only in his fourth year in the NBA, shouldn't be making that much money.

"It's like he's stealing money," he'd joke.

But after the game where Chris went for a season-high sixteen points in the Garden and his two-handed dunk from the baseline was on the front cover of the *New York Times* sports section, Obama eventually conceded that he might have been wrong about Duhon's potential and earnings.

"Your boy Duhon is killing it already," the president-elect said, approaching me, his face a sleepy grin. "Maybe he does deserve that money."

I agreed, and we shot the shit as we always did, recapping the games we'd watched, making our predictions for the NBA season, which was in full tilt, how great it was going to be with LeBron approaching free agency, and then, out of nowhere, he said, "You're coming with me, right?"

I thought I knew the answer to the question. Every fiber of my being was prepared to say, "not on this part of the journey." I had, in fact, already *said* no to everyone else on the team. And yet, in that instant, I somehow couldn't form the word. Instead, I took a deep breath and somehow blurted out, "Yeah, I'm in."

The president-elect gave me a fist dap, and that was that. I was back in the fold.

In the hours that followed, it dawned on me that maybe prior to that moment I'd been a little irrational, I'd been thinking about the job in the wrong way. And if nothing else, there was so much I knew I'd have missed out on. The team would have carried on, and I wouldn't have been there. You don't play all season and then punk out for the playoffs. That felt wrong. But not as wrong as saying no to the guy who was three months away from being the leader of the free world. As tired as I was at the end of the campaign and as ambivalent as I was about spending years in any capacity in government, I couldn't let him down now.

In the end, there was no way to decline. I was caught up in the mo. And it was going to take me where it wanted me to go.

★ ★ ★

The day of the inauguration, Tuesday, January 20, 2009, started just as so many others had on the campaign trail. There was a podium check. Obama wasn't making major changes to the speech, as he had in the past, but he was making small edits, and I was responsible for making certain they were entered in the final draft and on the teleprompter. I was the guy who could distinguish his "L's" from his "I's." Thankfully, the President's handwriting isn't messy, though he does prefer cursive, which can cause confusion. As can his habit of inserting chunks of text with arrows. But I'd had two years of practice deciphering his code.

It didn't escape me that, unlike our other events, this one was about to change the world forever: the inauguration of the first African-American president. Seven million citizens were projected to show up to watch history unfold and listen to him speak. People were sleeping in their cars because the hotels had sold out. The city had closed the bridges into the nation's capital; they were shutting down the town. It was like you see in a science-fiction movie when they literally pull up the bridges to keep more people from flooding into the city. All this historic insanity was swirling around me, but I still had a job to do, so I kept my head in the game and shut out the noise, way too busy to have a moment of reflection.

The chaos of the day was further compounded by the fact that I was new to my job at the White House. There were a million details that required tending to on that front, and on top of that, I'd just bought my first place, a seven-hundred-square-foot condo. I was sleeping on a mattress on the floor. My stuff was packed into boxes. I felt like I was treading water across the board, again.

The Obamas were staying at Blair House, the traditional residence for presidents-elect. Security had been amped up to epic proportions; it was even a challenge for me to get Obama's barber, Zariff, into the building so Obama could have his pre-inauguration trim. The motorcade to the Capitol was massive. There was no way any of us could have prepared ourselves for the transition. And yet, once you are in the flow of the shift, you find yourself floating right along. You deal.

So much of the inauguration was a blur, but what stands out in my memory is the minutes before Obama walked out to take his oath. Gibbs, Marvin, Mrs. Obama, the girls, and I were all in the holding area. One by one their names were called and they left to greet the crowds. Soon enough, it was just Marvin, the President, and me, standing in the background, the whole world eagerly waiting for him to appear on the platform. I remember we joked about how freezing it was outside, a record low. There we were, on the brink of a new life, a new *world order*, talking about the weather.

"How cold do you think it will be by the time I actually deliver the speech?" the president-elect asked.

"Not as cold as Springfield," I said. "And this time there's a heater under the podium. It'll be fine."

"Remember Springfield?" he said, smiling. I laughed. Springfield was where he'd announced his candidacy. It was February 2007, and the weather that day had been equally inhospitable. "It's going to be even colder than that," Obama said now.

"Yeah," I joked. "Colder and a little more crowded."

Soon, the Lincoln Bible was brought out, and the president-elect looked at the Good Book, then at himself in the mirror.

"It's all good," I said. "You got it." Fist bump and out, as his name was announced and he walked out onto the platform and made history.

I stayed behind and observed from the background. I saw the sea of overjoyed people and it stole my breath away. Finally, it washed over me. The significance of electing the first African-American president. What that meant to people like my grandparents. To the children around the world watching. And there I was, in the middle of it all, doing my part, as I had been all along.

20

HISTORY HAPPENS EVERY DAY

I had about as much prep for my transition into the West Wing as I did when I began my stint as bodyman. Which is to say: none. There was no *White House for Dummies* manual, not even a simple punch list. I did have the phone numbers of a few past presidential PAs—Jared Weinstein, Kris Engskov, Doug Band, Andrew Friendly—and I relied on their wisdom, particularly Jared Weinstein, a Duke alum '03, who had worked for Bush and gave me the best advice, which was really more of a warning.

"Something amazing will happen every day," he told me. What he meant was that being the personal aide to a sitting president was like watching the finale of the fireworks display every hour. It was as exhausting as it was phenomenal. He also said, "You're going to see a bunch of crazy shit. Stay composed anyway."

On Obama's second trip to D.C. during the transition, there was a lunch scheduled for all the personal aides of former presidents. Clinton's guy, Bush's guy, Carter's guy, Bush senior's guy. Do the math. Forty-four presidents. Only a few men in history had done this job. Sitting in the Ward Room down in the Navy Mess with these interesting and distinguished men regaling me with tales of what it's like to work as an aide to a president was when it hit me like a ton of bricks: *Special is an understatement and not many people ever have the chance to do it!*

After the inauguration, President Obama's team began taking up their offices in the White House. Though I'd visited the White House before, it was never as an employee whose office sat five steps from the Oval. Once there, my eyes darted to and fro, hungry to take everything in. I noted the grandfather clock in the corner, the star-burst rug left over from Bush (no one could see the point in replacing it when some Americans were barely making enough money to cover their rent). I marveled at the eagle carved into the ceiling of the Oval, its claws clutching the olive branch and the arrows, representing war and peace. Absorbing the weight and significance of the setting, I thought to myself, *Don't screw this up, Reggie.*

There was no rookie seminar class or debriefing. The only briefing that I got was when the White House curator took POTUS, FLOTUS, and me on a tour the first weekend. And that wasn't even on the schedule. The President decided, "I'm going to live here. When people ask me questions, I want to know the answers." I agreed one hundred percent. If I was working there, I should at least know something about the place.

The curator, Bill Allman, was visibly excited. He took the three of us on a five-hour exploration of every inch of the White House. You know when you are processing so much detail you can't keep it all in your head? That was the tour. Who created every piece of art, where the china came from, who chose what wallpaper. The kids joined us for a bit, but they grew weary and peeled away. Meanwhile, the President was asking an endless series of questions, eating up all the minutiae. And for the curator, it was like winning the lottery. I had the impression that no other president had ever asked for a tour before. I also got the impression that Obama understood that the White House was a museum. And he wanted to pay his respects.

In time, just as I had on the campaign, I found my professional groove. My typical day at the Oval saw me getting up between 5:15 and 5:45 A.M., going to the gym by myself, working out for forty-five minutes, showering, eating hard-boiled eggs, and walking ten minutes to arrive at the office between 7:30 and 8:00 A.M. I would sit in my office, go through the schedule, read all the briefings, make sure that I was aware of all the things that were happening throughout the day, become somewhat knowledgeable about the subjects on the off chance that he would say, "Hey, what's this?" or "Who is that?"

Reading the daily briefing book was my favorite part of the job. I learned so much. It was like going to college and majoring in everything. Economic reports, issues for advocacy groups, background on members of Congress, where they were from, how many children they had—I literally sat at the information hub of the world.

The President would arrive at the Oval Office around 8:30 or 9 A.M., after which there would be a PDB, "Presidential Daily Briefing," given by the national security team. As he was being briefed, usually his next appointment would be milling around the outer Oval, which meant milling around near my office. While they waited, I'd ask the financial experts what they thought was going to happen—how was the economy doing and why, what did they think the job numbers were going to be, were we seeing growth, what was the GDP? I'd talk to the military guys about Iraq. I'd talk to the legislative team about what was happening with the health care bill. It was a tremendous opportunity, and I seized it. Instead of sitting idly by and saying nothing, I used that time to educate myself about what was unfolding in the world. I also forged relationships that will prove useful in the future. I took advantage of the situation, instead of being intimidated; because I wasn't as seasoned or knowledgeable as most of the people being ushered in and out of the Oval, I asked questions. Jared was right. History was happening every day. And I made sure I was present for it.

★ ★ ★

I also learned quickly that being in the White House basically means you are always moments away from the next crisis. Every day brings another storm, and you have to batten down and brave the weather. The buck stops with the President.

POTUS felt the weight of his office keenly. He would tell me, "All the easy problems have already been solved before they come to me." The folks surrounding him excelled at their jobs. They knew what they were doing. So if any problem made its way to the Oval Office, that meant it was a doozy, and often these problems required immediate solutions.

I made it a facet of my job to find the silver lining in the day-to-day activities, even if I had to make it up. "Look here, sir. Between 2:20 and 2:45 you have a window." He would often use these small moments to grab a chance to see an old friend. They'd swing by the Oval, and in those brief windows of time, he'd smile, say something like, "It's been way too long. How old are your kids now?"

Sometimes the friend's children came, too. As he did with everyone, Obama always interacted with them, no matter how young. All in all, it was the normalcy in what was otherwise a full and demanding schedule.

★ ★ ★

Once I was settled into my cubbyhole office a few feet from the Oval, in theory I had fewer duties then I'd had on the campaign, but the

Playing basketball with President Obama at St. Bart's Church in New York City, during downtime, Sept. 23, 2009.

The president-elect walking out to his inauguration on January 20, 2009.

Me on the National Mall on Inauguration Day, 2009.

View from the Capitol during the inaugural ceremony.

President Barack Obama and I fist bump as Chief of Staff Rahm Emanuel looks on, in the Oval Office, June 16, 2009.

In the Oval Office, me with the President, First Lady, and my parents, January 23, 2009.

In the Oval Office—March 15, 2011.

In the corner while POTUS waits to speak at an opening session of the White House Forum on Jobs and Economic Growth, December 3, 2009.

Walking back to the Oval Office after Nick Saban and the Alabama Crimson Tide visit the White House.

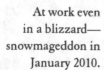

At work even in a blizzard— snowmageddon in January 2010.

Looking through the peephole in the door to the Oval Office, January 27, 2009.

Walking with President Obama along the colonnade of the White House, December 3, 2009.

scale of them went way up. I was still responsible for helping with the execution of Obama's daily schedule and its logistics. For anything that was planned at the White House, I would need to know the specifics, the duration, the details. Then, when we traveled off-site, it was more like the old days of the campaign—only with triple the entourage and details. (The Executive Office protocol seemed cumbersome to me. When I wanted to decorate the wall of my office with a framed copy of the Duke newspaper carrying the headline "2010 National Champions," I had to get an approval letter, a signature, and talk to three different people in different departments before a single nail was hammered. I guess that was to be expected when your office is part of a museum.)

On the road, Marvin or I would tell the President what to expect for the day—the number of people in a photo line, the crowd size for a speech, etc. During the campaign, Sean Graham-White, or someone from his team, typically had been the teleprompter operator. But during the presidency, there was a team from the White House Communications Agency—an operator, a deputy, and a technician—and they handled their job to perfection, which made work for me easier.

Other dimensions of my job were made simpler. With the presidency came perks. There was always food on hand. There were printers everywhere; bottled water, chilled and not chilled. I still loved the job, but suddenly there was a lot more support. And my responsibility was more to manage the support, instead of doing the tasks myself. Sounds great, but it came with complications and a new learning curve.

Before working in the West Wing, if Obama wanted to speak to someone on the phone, he would just pick up the phone and dial, or I would just pass him my cell phone with the line connected. I would open every single call with, "Hello, I'm Reggie Love, I have Senator Obama here and he would like to speak with you." Once in the White House, there were teams dedicated to placing secure and nonsecure phone calls. I didn't have to figure out where meals were going to come from because now there was the Navy Mess with its professional chefs. When POTUS ate out, I would just have to communicate the plan, location, and time, and someone else would make it happen. I was learning to expect the unexpected, seamlessly.

Now and again, I found myself babysitting the kids of visiting dignitaries. Like when French president Nicolas Sarkozy and his wife, Carla Bruni, came to the White House for dinner. They brought President Sarkozy's twelve-year-old son, Louis, along because he wanted to meet the Obama girls, but Sasha and Malia weren't home, so it fell to me to entertain him.

I showed Louis around the White House, the swimming pool, the garden. He enjoyed himself, and when it was all over, Sarkozy collected him and gave me a hug. (Something he's continued to do every time I have seen him since.) The fact that he even knows who I am is incredible enough. But a ritual hug? Even I couldn't dream that up.

While my new position could be fun, it remained odd to go from having so much autonomy to being a manager. I'd grown accustomed to the frantic pace and ceaseless workload of the campaign. A part of me longed for that energy again. In the Oval, I had a desk job. It was a stellar location, of course. But it was still a desk.

There was a tangible shift in my job and my relationship with everyone working around me. It reminded me of when my basketball team would disband after the season. You grow addicted to the heightened camaraderie and closeness of a team with a single, shared goal. There was also a subtle shift in my accountability, a shift from representing a candidate and a campaign to representing a president and a country.

The transition to the White House was tough on other people, too. For instance, the first lady used to say she wished she could sneak out and go shopping. Just hit the mall and browse a store or two. But, of course, she couldn't. Not without tons of security and then being mobbed when she arrived. Being in D.C. and living in the White House bubble meant that people had to adapt to feeling somewhat trapped.

Even the basketball games changed. When I organized them, they were now basketball games with the President, major events, not an Election Day ritual that Marvin would try to dodge.

There were upsides to the new routine. For one, I got parts of my personal life back. I was able to date more often. I also had time to think about what was next, to start looking into getting an MBA or a law degree. The WallyBag stayed in the closet more often than not, and I had an apartment, kitchen, and bed I could return to no matter how late the day ran. But none of that compared to the adrenaline rush of the campaign trail. I remember reading a psychological study that found that the more grueling an experience is, the more enlivening your memory of that experience will be. If you manage to summit Everest, you're not going to forget it. I hated Iowa. I hated the cold. I hated so much about the campaign. And yet I oddly missed it, like Stockholm syndrome. When we would return to Iowa, I would always want to swing by the old Hampton Inn and the gym tucked away close by in the strip mall.

Though my duties altered in scope, I knew I retained value in the President's eyes, if for no other reason than familiarity. The White House was not an unknown just to me, but also to him. And no matter what, he knew he could trust me. Beyond that, I was the only other brother working on the first floor of the West Wing, in the bubble every day.

All told, we'd won. We had bested the campaign's challenges, delivered a new and unfamiliar message, and we were finally in a position to start making good on promises.

What I hadn't fully realized was that the win was only the

beginning. It wasn't the summit, but the start of an even more arduous climb. We'd pushed ourselves to the limit to achieve this amazing goal, but once we did, the clouds cleared and all you could see was more mountains still to climb. There would be no relaxing, no victory dance. In actuality, the job was just beginning. The campaign had been historic, but what it had bought was the opportunity to make history. Every day.

21

CHARACTER COUNTS IN LARGE AMOUNTS

Working in the Outer Oval was a true honor. It also came with a fair amount of absurdity. Unlike in sports, where stats and wins are clear and measurable, with politics, the wins are often intangible. That ambiguity leads to an institution-wide insecurity. People find themselves battling for recognition and measuring their self-worth by whether or not they get invited to a holiday party, or are acknowledged in a speech, or given a birthday card, or asked to watch a basketball game.

In D.C., those goofy social arrangements have an impact on how people view you, and how people view your relationship with them. Forget fame—in Washington, people chase power. And some people grow jealous if they see others ascending along the road of perceived influence faster than themselves.

I'd been conditioned to the sports world, where if you're the squeaky wheel, you get cut. But more often than not in politics, the squeaky wheel gets greased. There are, of course, politics and out-sized personalities off the court in sports, but for a team to win consis-tently, those issues become distant concerns after tip-off. Washington, however, has no such clearly marked lines, and the politics bled into everything. Merit is far from the only reason people get anything of perceived value. All of this was a big unfamiliar lesson for me, and watching the skill with which Obama navigated it was an education.

The President, while adept at handling that culture of insincerity and political maneuvering, was never a part of it. He came in as an outsider—he ran and won on that difference—and as such, he was able to stay above the fray. I was not always as successful.

Even before we got to Washington, I remember riding in the car when the candidate got off the phone with then President Bush. Bush was trying to round up Democrats in Congress to get TARP (the Troubled Asset Relief Program) passed. We were in a motorcade in San Francisco, and after the senator hung up, I said, "I know it isn't my place to comment on this, but why would you support this? The Republicans would never help the Democrats in a situation like this. And doesn't it make your chances of winning better if the Republi-cans are shown to be totally out of control?"

Senator Obama looked me in the eye and said, "What's most im-portant are the people who are going to be most affected by having a lack of access to capital, small businesses unable to make payroll or to have working capital to fill orders. The people responsible for this mess won't suffer nearly as bad as the people least responsible for it."

He wasn't trying to calculate the benefit the financial crisis might have on his campaign. He was pained for the Americans he knew would endure hardship. That was the problem crying out for a solu-tion; if he could help, he would, and he did. Unlike many of the Republicans today and during that first term, Obama didn't believe in being an obstructionist. This was a philosophy he adhered to even as a junior senator from Illinois, where he advised the Democrats not to filibuster the confirmation of Judge Alito or, despite his public misgivings about it, the reauthorization of the Patriot Act.

"Give it an up or down vote. Don't take advantage of the process," he said.

This was a real lesson for me as someone who had always focused on scores and rankings—who was up, who was down, who lost, who won. As an athlete, I thought I knew what victory looked like. But in a great many domains, I learned that sometimes you win by losing. Or in Obama's case, that it was worth the risk of forfeiting a temporary political opportunity to serve the greater good.

I'll admit, the post-election power grab by every Tom, Dick, and Harry made me a bit nuts. I soon learned that for many people clamoring to get appointments, face time with the President was more valuable than actually doing their job. When you meet people in Washington, the first thing they want to know is what you do and who *you* know. Everyone wants to see who can pee the farthest.

This always struck me as silly. Having spent time with several triumphant athletic franchises, and a few struggling ones, and been a part of a groundbreaking grassroots presidential campaign, I had learned time and again that every player and every play matters. In any organization, every piece has value. A house won't stay standing without a sturdy foundation. Or to use a sports metaphor: one man can't do it all and can't play every position on the court; you need an entire team to win.

This wisdom seemed scarce in ball-hogging Washington, where certain people derived value from being able to *say* their job was important. It was as if they stopped at passion and forgot about performance, confused being on a winning team with actually contributing to its success. Often times, it seemed to me that in government, no one loved you until they thought you could do something for them. It reminded me of being back in high school, where the pretty girl ignores you until you make the team, and then suddenly she wants you to take her to prom.

POTUS handled the nonsense with grace. He was used to standing tall in the face of small-minded people. Me? I had to learn. Though I wasn't explicitly told my new responsibilities, I sussed out in the face of this new interpersonal Oval dynamic that one of them was to be the guy who said "No." I was the opposite of a yes man. I was the no man. I would be respectful, polite, accommodating. I would respond in a timely, gracious fashion. But in the end, on the majority of asks that poured in like ants to a pile of sugar, I had to offer an apologetic "No."

Not only was I the no man, I had to make the people I said no to feel as if they had been told yes. The social interaction needed to be pleasant. And that required a mastery of tact—not, I concede, my strongest suit going into my new position.

There was one guy whose only reason for being seemed to be to play a round of golf with the President. And he would email me weekly to remind me of that fact. I responded, courteously, that though the President was flattered, playing golf with this clearly sincere admirer currently was not a possibility for the commander in chief. Then this man began sending emails about how he read that Obama was playing golf with other people, and if he had time to do that, he should have time to play with him. His emails became more and more audacious, but I could only thank him for his support and friendship. Those were the rules. He could cross a line. I could not.

The only thing worse than saying no was saying yes. When I granted a request, I needed to have done as much vetting of the person and the appeal as humanly possible. Was there precedence for this request? Was this something we could actually accommodate? What were the implications if we did? How would saying yes to this look to the outside world? I needed to avoid anything that suggested special treatment, because if I said yes to one thing, you could bet several dozen people would file right behind wanting the same consideration. Any yes opened the floodgates to copycat requests.

When I did grant a request, I would hear complaints such as "I did more for Obama than that person," or "I've known the President longer," or "Why did they get that option and we didn't?"

Playing gatekeeper wasn't the most fun I could have in a day. I was yelled at, hung up on, bullied, threatened, flirted with, and propositioned—sometimes all by the same person.

I would hear all about how when Bill Clinton was president, so and so got to do such and such. And my job was to keep this ridiculousness from reaching the President. I had to stay out in front of the hungry masses. And I needed to keep them happy as much as I could, without burdening his time. Part of my responsibility was making sure people felt like they were heard and appreciated. Making people feel connected was important to me and to the team. I did have *some* sway, but I used it judiciously, or so I hoped.

When I first started working in the White House, every time I met people socially, POTUS was, understandably, all anyone wanted to talk about. Whereas on the campaign trail, I was aware that my actions spoke for more than myself, once I was in the employ of the President, I realized that my own identity had been completely subsumed by the President and the Office. Everywhere I went, I became "the guy who plays basketball with the President." Imagine the questions you get when someone finds out you know, say, Oprah or Kanye West.

At times it made dating tough, when it was hard to know the motivations of the women who expressed interest. (On the plus side, I had the best "get out of jail" card you could invent. "I'd love to go to the ballet, but I've gotta work"—most people have no problem being second priority behind the President of the United States.)

A part of me consistently worried that others were involved with me for the wrong reasons. To have even a semblance of a normal social life, I had to learn how to trust. POTUS helped me to do this in ways he didn't realize. He showed me what true character looked like.

When Obama was elected he told me, "I'm commander in chief. I'm responsible for every soldier in our military." He decided to visit a military hospital every few months. He wanted to put a face on the bigger issues. As he generally did, he chose to humanize the problem, rather than distance himself via statistics or studies. It is possible to forget a detail in a briefing that lands on your desk. It is not so easy to forget the stories and staggering courage of our men and women who serve this great country, once they have told you about their lives and losses eye-to-eye.

POTUS was never one to shy away from the feelings behind a policy. Just as his mother's health struggles had fueled his desire to fight for the Affordable Care Act, his one-on-one time with wounded warriors at military hospitals and elsewhere inspired his commitment to the Department of Veterans Affairs. He took initiatives like the Recovery Act (which provided $1.4 billion to improve services for the department) and tax credits, and made a public promise to end veteran homelessness by 2015. Programs, incidentally, that as of 2012, had resulted in a 20 percent decrease in veteran unemployment compared with the prior year, and in 2013 saw a 23.49 percent reduction in veteran homelessness.

The President would tell me that when it came to our military, words of thanks and promises of help were not enough. He considered the lack of support veterans suffered a source of national shame. He believed they had committed for life and so should we as a country. That was something he and Coach K had in common: an unyielding devotion and gratitude to the men and women who risked everything to serve those of us at home. It remains a humbling touchstone for me as well. Whenever I feel sorry for myself, or begin to take for granted the liberties I have as a citizen, I think back to those times with the

President in the patient rooms of Walter Reed, or to the letters and photographs of servicemen and -women that Coach K used to show us at Duke when our team was out of touch with reality.

"This is what sacrifice looks like," Coach K would say, holding up pictures of soldiers. And he was right.

Just as I'd observed Obama do on the campaign, in Washington I aimed to understand the perspectives of all different kinds of people. Every day I intersected with people from various walks of life, and often from far-flung places around the world. In doing so, I soon learned how relative most of our perceptions and beliefs are, and how insignificant a space I actually occupied.

It was like that feeling you get when you look out your airplane window. The world is big. And you are so small. Being a part of an NCAA Championship team may have carried weight in my former social and professional circles, but to visiting diplomats from South Korea or Japan, my collegiate sports meant nothing. The same was true of my education and background.

It was a profound lesson to grasp that at the end of the day, the only thing that really defines you is how you conduct yourself human to human. Everything you might think distinguishes your identity—your appearance, your earnings, your lineage, your fame—are all reduced to sand when you intersect with someone from a completely foreign world. No one in Beirut cares that you attended Harvard. No one in the Sudan gives a flip about who your parents are. The only true international currency is character.

It was the same thing Coach K had drilled into me, and my father, too, since I was old enough to blow my own nose. It was an example Obama had set since the day we met: Character doesn't just count. It is the password to every code you will ever need to crack.

22

VALUE THE BALL

Know this: your world is a fishbowl. So you'd best keep it clean. And not just because it is always safer to assume that everyone eventually sees everything and nothing stays hidden for long. Far less appreciated is another truth: you never know who is going to swim back into your orbit.

Which brings to my mind December 13, 2007. We were in the thick of the hard, heated days of the early campaign, and I met Gibbs and Axelrod on the tarmac at Washington National to load up ahead of the candidate's arrival. Our flight attendant's last name was Stoner, and she was quite proud of her unusual moniker. The timing was comical. The previous day Billy Shaheen, cochair of Hillary Clinton's New Hampshire campaign, had publicly and pointedly raised Obama's youthful indiscretions with drug use, noting that the

GOP would use them to destroy the candidate in the general election. Clearly, Shaheen wasn't going to wait for the GOP to raise the issue. We were all standing outside discussing his press conference as the flight was being readied for takeoff when Huma Abedin, Clinton's personal aide, walked over to our plane and pulled me aside.

"My boss wants to talk to your boss," she said.

"Ooo-kay," I answered, reaching to ring the candidate, who, as it turned out, was pulling onto the tarmac at that moment. I told him Senator Clinton wanted a quick word, and he agreed as he exited the car. I joined him and we walked toward her plane. Senator Clinton emerged, reached the tarmac, and intercepted us halfway.

"I want to apologize for the whole Shaheen thing," she said. "I want you to know I had nothing to do with it."

The candidate very respectfully told her the apology was kind, but largely meaningless, given the emails it was rumored her camp had been sending out labeling him as a Muslim. Before he could finish his sentence, she exploded on Obama. In a matter of seconds, she went from composed to furious. It had not been Obama's intention to upset her, but he wasn't going to play the fool either. To all of us watching the spat unfold, it was an obvious turning point in our campaign, and we knew it. Clinton was no less competitive or committed to a cause than Obama, and the electric tension running through both candidates and their respective staffs reflected the understanding that she was no longer the de facto Democratic candidate. Her inevitability had been questioned.

After the skirmish, we all went back to our respective aircrafts to fly to Des Moines for yet another debate. The press had been forecasting that Senator Clinton was going to go for the throat, since she and Obama's campaign clashes had been getting national attention. In reality, the debate was dull until the last minute, when Carolyn Washburn, the then editor of the *Des Moines Register*, asked Senator

Obama how he could claim to be an agent of change when he had so many former Clinton advisors on his foreign policy team.

Clinton snorted and muttered, "I want to hear that."

Obama quickly and sharply responded, "Well, Hillary, I'm looking forward to you advising me as well."

The crowd exploded in laughter. Senator Clinton fell silent, and Senator Obama finished answering the question. That one line was the only news to come out of the whole event.

I remember Obama telling me later that day that he knew he was going to win the nomination after that moment on the tarmac, because Clinton had unraveled, and he was still standing and keeping his cool. It was just the confidence boost he needed.

During the primaries you would hear all these stories about how the HRC campaign was strong-arming people, or making jokes about Obama supporters. Contentious stuff. And yet we'd all be stuck in the same waiting areas and green rooms, so we'd end up talking to each other for hours at a time. There was nowhere else to go, and it seemed silly to stand there in silence pretending to hate each other.

As it goes in politics, once the senator was officially declared the Democratic nominee, the Clintons became huge assets and eventually friends to the Obamas and the campaign, and as we know, she became a formidable secretary of state.

After Clinton conceded in the primary, Huma and I went to dinner at this fancy Georgetown restaurant called Cafe Milano. She brought Anthony Weiner, and I brought a friend. The newspapers ended up writing a story about the meal, which was an out-of-body experience for me. I was now tabloid fodder, though it was probably more Anthony and Huma drawing the attention.

I also developed an enjoyable relationship with Hillary once Obama was in the White House and she was Madam Secretary. She was usually early to her weekly meeting with the President. While she waited, she'd ask me questions about my life, traveling, my family. I always tried to ask questions in turn about what was going on internationally. A result I'm sure of having been first lady, a U.S. senator, and now secretary of state, her command of facts was astounding. She was formidable because she'd had to be.

I met President Clinton for the first time during the campaign. He was traveling through DCA the same day we were. I was waiting in the lobby of Signature Aviation with Marvin when the former president came over with his aide Doug Band to introduce himself. He shook my hand and said, "Hey, how are you doin'?" like he'd known me all his life.

Doug then turned to Marvin and explained to Clinton how Marvin had been the bodyman for Kerry, but Clinton seemed to know all of this already. He smiled, seemed interested and personable, then suggested in his happy Southern drawl that we pose for a photograph.

I was torn. Should I take a picture with Bill Clinton while my candidate was running against his wife? What if the photo got leaked? How would that look? What if the whole thing was a setup?

Then again, he was a former president, and if a former president is standing there saying, "Hey, let's take a picture!" you can't really shrug and say, "Nah, no thanks."

The whole thing was incredibly awkward, at least for me. President Clinton, it seemed, had never seen an awkward moment in his life.

I posed for the picture.

Knowing President Clinton a bit better now, and having seen how hard he campaigned for Obama, I know he is an amazing guy, unbelievably sharp, with a great sense of humor. He cares deeply about the country, especially about the middle class. With politicians, you often get either someone who is very smart or someone who is very down to earth. You rarely get both. Clinton and Obama happen to be both. Clinton basically wrote the book on folksy genius and connecting with every demographic. Obama is his own brand, but the DNA is similar. These are men who were forged in adversity and have not left their upbringing behind.

Nor have they allowed their roots to define who they would become. They dreamed big, even as many of those in their hometown communities could not. They truly represent the best of both worlds.

Being an athlete early on in life taught me not just teamwork, but the ability to be coached. Trusting a coach to know better than you teaches you to listen to other people's advice. If nothing else, a coach prepares you for humility. And that is as valuable a lesson as any in life.

★ ★ ★

When I first moved to D.C., I realized very quickly how fundamentally screwed up the professional Washington bureaucratic system was. The cost of living *far* outpaced the average entry-level salary. So in order to work in D.C. politics or government, you needed either to be wealthy or to know the right people, and then you probably had to live in Southern Maryland or Northern Virginia. To get into the world, you already had to be *in* the world—a paradox that excluded a large percentage of Americans the government supposedly represents.

I was lucky to find a way in through the back door. I had played a little football, I had some money saved, and I didn't have any burdening undergraduate student loans (I wish I could say the same about business school). When you are just getting out of college, most people who look like me don't have the financial flexibility to come live in D.C. on a staff assistant's salary.

Obama understood that. Which is one reason why when he was a junior senator he started his PAC, the Hope Fund, part of which paid for a diverse group of young people to come to D.C. and train for a political career. The Hope Fund participants worked campaigns, took seminars, met with politicos and policy wonks. A large percentage of the graduates from the program eventually ended up working on the '08 campaign. I remember picking up some of these newbies from the airport and seeing their eyes light up as we drove into D.C. It was so rewarding to play a part in their introduction to Washington, their anticipation and eagerness much like my own when I had arrived not too long before.

I respected Obama for his creation of that small program as much as for anything else he did. He saw something wrong with the system. He understood why it was broken. And then he created a new structure to address the imbalance and begin paving a path to success for a whole new group of people. He knew the ship could not be righted overnight, but he did something concrete to begin the process. He made an actual difference; the seeds he sowed almost immediately took root.

It made me think of something Coach K used to tell us every practice, which was "Value the ball." In a game where you have fifty to seventy possessions, you need to value every single one of them, because you never know which one will mean the difference in the final score.

In ways large and small, Obama valued the ball and respected every possession. Here's one unheralded example. Unlike past presidents, President Obama didn't want to cancel White House tours when he came to the Oval Office on weekends. I was told by Secret Service that if George W. Bush went into the Oval on a Saturday, they would shut down the whole West Wing. But Obama felt strongly about not disrupting people's long-held plans and schedules. Instead, he popped his head out and said hi to folks. He shook hands with friends and families who were touring the West Wing. He stayed as grounded and accessible as one can be as the leader of the free world.

One of my tasks in the White House was to log the gifts. It was mind-boggling the amount of stuff that poured in for the Obama family. Basketballs, shoes, iPads, flowers, photographs—I would categorize them and track the thank-you notes we sent in return. I never wanted the President to run into someone who'd given him a present and had not received an acknowledgment. Good manners and character go hand in hand.

Which brings me back to the fishbowl or, in the case of D.C., the shark tank. The President showed me via his own choices that you have to value everyone's contribution, from the grandma sending a birthday card to the Hollywood comedian writing a million-dollar donation. And never discount what someone may someday bring to the table. Politics cannot help but be personal, sometimes even nasty. Political success, however, is not measured in personalities, but in accomplishments. Just as a team of prima donnas is a long, long shot to win a championship, an administration or, for that matter, a political party that cannot join together for the greater good of the country is doomed to come up short.

23

MOTHERS KNOW BEST

The most valuable gift the women in my life have given me is empathy.
A newfound sensitivity that came in handy in the White House,
where you have to give every individual with a grievance as much
time as he or she needs to feel heard. You listen to people and you nod
and you listen some more, until *they* know that *you* know the depth
of their disappointment. My sensitivity training was usually at someone's expense, sadly, after I'd messed up by being a lousy boyfriend,
a bad friend, or a bratty son. So I had to be enlightened. Repeatedly.
Often this was via a heated phone call I received while I sat in the
back row of a Suburban with Obama, Secret Service, and anyone else
traveling with us. Often those calls were at volumes loud enough for
Obama (and everyone else in a five-mile radius) to overhear. Nothing

quite like being dressed down by a woman scorned in front of your boss while he's pretending not to listen.

Over time, the candidate, then the President, met a select few of my serious girlfriends. Every interaction was fraught for me. I mean, "Let me introduce you to the President of the United States" is about the best line a guy could possibly have in his pocket. But then they would actually *meet* the President, and how was I ever going to top that?

★ ★ ★

The first lady was no less eager to dispense romantic counsel, but at least her approach was more maternal.

"Who are you dating? Is it serious?" she'd ask me. "Do you think she's a good person?" She wanted me to find a nice girl and settle down. She viewed me as part of the Obama family. And as a person who maybe needed a little guidance. She always advised me to make sure the person I ended up with was self-possessed, someone whose whole world didn't revolve around me.

"Get a strong, smart, independent woman," she'd say.

When she said that, I'd think about my own mother, Lynette Love.

Born November 24, 1952, my mother grew up in the segregated South during the Jim Crow era. Her high school, Moultrie High, was integrated just three years prior to her attending. As it was a racially polarizing time, the integration was less than smooth. Even so, my mother was never bitter about her history. Instead, she was determined. She labored to change the future, volunteering for local African-American candidates, like Harvey Gantt, the first African-American mayor of Charlotte.

"You have to forgive," she'd tell me, "but never forget."

To make sure *I* didn't forget, she gave me civil rights reading assignments. The idea of wasting a warm summer day in North

Carolina with my head buried in a book and not shooting hoops was the craziest thing I could imagine. I'd complain, "Why am I learning about Fredrick Douglass and W. E. B. Du Bois? I'm not in school. I want to play basketball."

And she would tell me that nothing held any value unless you knew the story behind it, and that any story of my life included those great men and I was lucky for it. So I read, and learned.

My mother was consistently strict, but fair. She never spanked me—that was my father's job—but make no mistake, she was intimidating, nonetheless. She held me and my brother to the highest behavioral and academic standards and never accepted any excuse for our not meeting them.

After my lackluster performance in middle school, my mother led the charge of *Operation Get Reggie Love to Private School*. She knew I could rise to the challenge, even if I didn't know it. I was unfocused and a poor test taker, but my mother saw a brighter future for me if I could just overcome those hurdles. I took remedial classes to catch up and learned strategies for improving my concentration. I wasn't going to fail, because my mother wasn't going to let me fail. Ironically, in 2012, thirteen years after I graduated from Providence Day, a school that hadn't even been sure they wanted me to attend, I was asked to deliver their commencement address. I was proud, but my mother was even prouder.

While my mom was pushing me to be a better man and high achiever, she was herself making strides. She worked in HR at Philip Morris for nearly twenty years, one of the few African-American women in their employ at the time, after which she left to start her own business in 1995. She bought a building in the heart of West Charlotte, only a mile down the road from our Friendship Baptist missionary church. She turned it into commercial real estate space, and named it the Elise Jackson Professional Building after my grandmother. She converted one of the bottom-floor units into a hair salon, which she dubbed the Classy Look Salon, a thriving business she managed herself. My mother was a workhorse, and she expected the same of her sons. It was great preparation for Duke, for the campaign, and for life.

This is not to say we didn't have our mother-son conflicts. One of the biggest came during the first presidential inauguration.

My parents wanted to attend, so I called my mom and said, "Great news! I have a dozen tickets. I don't care who you invite, or what you do with them, but here are the instructions. Just understand there are no more tickets after that."

And then she went and invited more than a dozen people, conveniently overlooking the dilemma of lodging. Washington is filled for any inauguration, but the historic inauguration of the country's first African-American president meant every possible room was spoken for. I'd rented a room at a house for my parents, and I had my one-bedroom condo. But that was the extent of the crash-pad space.

"Look, Ma, you and Dad can stay at the place that I reserved. It's nice, it's close to the Capitol. You can literally walk from the house to the inauguration."

And she was like, "Wonderful. I'm also bringing about six friends and cousins."

It was insane. I think she believed because I was close to the President, I could work some sort of miracle. Which I could not.

"Relax, Reggie," my mom said in that voice all parents use when they are trying to calm their children down. "This is a historic time. You're just too close to it. People will be happy sleeping on the floor."

I felt overwhelmed. I was running around trying to figure out my new job with the president-elect and also manage my folks and their friends. I did the best I could for the hometown gang, but every time I dropped by to visit, I felt like I was somehow letting one or all of them down. I tried to explain the position I felt she was putting me into, but my mom wouldn't hear my whining.

★ ★ ★

That week, Obama inquired as to how my parents were doing. I wrinkled my nose.

"Ugh," I said. "They're here. I can say that." Then I launched into my litany of complaints about how much of a pain they were being.

The president was unsympathetic. In fact, he was annoyed.

"Reggie, you never know how long your parents are going to be around," he began. "So you should take every moment that you have to appreciate your parents and do the right thing for them. There is not a day that goes by that I don't wish my mother was still alive."

His words hit me like a bucket of cold water. I had been so wrapped up in how exasperating I thought my mom was acting, I didn't think about what this inauguration meant for her, a woman who not only had strived to help support our family, but also had been such a pioneer for black women in our community. Just as she had tried to teach me way back when I was a kid reading MLK and Malcolm X, all our stories were connected. Hers, mine, the President's, and the stories of all the other African-Americans who had preceded us in much harsher circumstances. We were all part of the same narrative, and to rob her of joy in this moment suddenly seemed, in light of what Obama had explained to me, churlish and ungrateful.

"Invite your mother for a visit," he insisted.

I demurred. I didn't even know the process to get security clearance for a trip to the Oval. Obama side-eyed me.

"Reggie, I am the President of the United States. Invite your parents over here because I would like to see the Love family while they are still in town."

Chastened, I went and found my mom and apologized. Then I took her and my dad to the Oval Office to meet the Obamas.

The President and the first lady embraced them warmly and told my parents how I was "like a son" to them. Mrs. Obama bragged about me, told them I was "amazing." Obama said he couldn't imagine being at the White House without me. My mother was over the moon. To have the first family saying to my family that we were *all* family—it doesn't really get any better than that.

I remember my mom was wearing these green leather pants. She looked nuts to me, but the Obamas complimented them. When my parents left, Obama turned to me and said, "That wasn't so hard, was it?"

The next day my mom and I were walking past the Washington Monument when she linked her arm in mine. We talked about the inauguration, meeting the Obamas, the wonder of everything she'd just been a part of.

"If only your grandmother could have been here to see this," my mom said, her eyes welling with tears. "She would never believe it." She stopped for a second, straightened my tie, and patted my chest. "You don't realize how blessed you are."

As we started walking again, she took my hand. And I thought, *I'm starting to, Mom. I'm starting to.*

24

DON'T BE AFRAID TO LAUGH AT YOURSELF

Like most young men with a healthy ego, I used to take myself a bit too seriously. I was big on swallowing my feelings, putting up a front, and generally being as untouchable as I could make myself. Like a lot of my teenage friends, I figured striking a pose was far better than admitting a weakness, and might even cover for one. Back then, my ability to welcome criticism was a muscle I hadn't yet figured out how to exercise.

This was before I learned the value of being able to laugh not only at life, but, more critically, at myself. I was helped on my road to enlightenment by the campaign team—by their gallows humor and shared propensity for making me the butt of as many jokes as they could manage.

As for the hazing, I made it easy for them in New Hampshire.

It was a snowy day, as usual, and I was catching a ride in one of the Secret Service armored Suburbans. Typically the agents would occupy the last row of seats, which faced out toward the road like the seats in an old station wagon from the seventies. This allowed them to more easily see behind us.

The positioning of the seats also meant that you couldn't enter or exit the vehicle without somebody else opening the hatch for you like a trunk, and even then, you had to scramble like you were going through an obstacle course. And so, there I was, folding all six feet, four and three-quarter inches of me into the back of the Suburban, wearing a tie, sport coat, and trusty gray pants—pants I had planned to wear a couple of times that week, mind you—when I heard the distinctive sound of fabric tearing. Shredding, more accurately. This was not a minor seam pull. This was a full-on split. My whole backside was exposed, what remained of my pants hanging loosely beside my boxers like curtains.

It was 6 P.M., and we were on our way to the last campaign stop of the day. I called Eric Lesser, who was then doing advance in New Hampshire.

"Eric, I need my suitcase," I whispered into the phone as I exited the Suburban and waddled to the town hall event, one hand grasping what was left of my pants together behind me.

Eric said he'd do his best, but he was busy and I was busy as well, and what that ended up meaning was that I attended the town hall with my butt hanging out.

This little incident was fodder for jokes until the end of the New Hampshire primary, especially with the senator, who thought it was hilarious. Accidents and gaffes of this nature were no stranger to me throughout my five-year marathon with him.

Another such blunder occurred after the election, during the transition period. We were flying to Ohio to visit a factory, and then we were going to Philadelphia to meet Vice President Biden. It was piercingly cold outside.

When you begin a campaign, you usually start without a plane. You are on a United flight out of Concourse A at Reagan National Airport, with peanuts and pretzels if you are lucky. As the campaign gathers steam and funds, and the demands on the candidate's time increase, you graduate to cramped charter planes. Then you get Secret Service and you need more room and one flight attendant. Then the campaign needs a press pool and you move to a 757 or 747, which has an entire team of flight attendants. Some crew members were with us for months at a time, and we became close friends. Tracy Nuzzo must have traveled with us for almost six consecutive months during the primaries, and then Aiyana Knowles and her team carried the load through the last several months of the general election. I was probably the only person who really had a vested interest in the crew, as they were integral to my coordinating hundreds of in-flight meals, magazines, and newspapers—not to mention convincing the pilots to radio mid-flight to find out the score of the Bulls and Bears game or the NCAA Tournament upsets.

During the presidential transition, there was a new plane assigned and a whole new crew, which was a bummer, because I loved the familiarity of the old gang. It felt relaxing having folks on board who knew the team and knew the drill—whether we were nappers or nervous fliers or wanted extra lemon in our water, or whatever.

And so we boarded the plane with the new set of flight attendants, who were working really hard to make a good first impression. Soon enough, they started coming down the aisles, handing out all this food and drink, newspapers, blankets. I explained I didn't want anything, thank you very much. But they persisted. I repeated, "Really, I'm fine, I'm fine."

Between you and me, I had a thing about eating on planes. I was always afraid I was going to get food poisoning and become violently ill while on some cross-country flight, and for me it just wasn't worth the risk. I had a couple of colleagues who spent most of a cross-country and then an overseas trip inside a miniscule toilet stall. So, unless I was starving, I never ate on a plane, and if I did eat, I always went with the safe options—bread, cereal, rice, chicken. This meant no fish, no curries, nothing risky.

Still, the flight attendants kept pushing their meals and snacks on me. I kept turning them down, and I felt like I was coming off as a jerk. They didn't know me the way the old crew did, or my no-meals-on-flights philosophy. Meanwhile, everyone else on board was happily accepting this and that and otherwise having a grand old chow-down time.

"They think you don't like them," Marvin said in between bites of his lunch.

"That's ridiculous," I answered, sighing.

He chided me. "Just take something to be polite."

By now it was the dessert course. One of the new attendants stopped by my seat and gave me the rundown.

"We have cheesecake, cookies, fresh fruit, and we have these artisanal popsi—"

"I'm okay," I interrupted her.

Marvin chimed in to the flight attendant, "Tough crowd today," referring to me and my disinterest in the items being served. "Sometimes Reg is just cranky."

"Fine." I caved. "I'll have a cherry popsicle."

I quickly opened up the wrapper and popped the frozen dessert in my mouth, simultaneously saying, "Mmmm, it's great, thank you so much," and making a big show of the popsicle being the tastiest treat I'd ever had in my life—and before the attendant could even roll her cart away, the entire thing had adhered itself to my face and lips.

You know that idiot kid who sticks his tongue on the flag pole outside in the middle of winter? That was me, only I was on a plane with our team, a press pool, and the president-elect, and let's not forget, we were on our way to the first public event outside of Chicago since Election Day.

"Excuse me," I tried to say through paralyzed lips. "I, I can't get this thing off me."

"Pardon?" the attendant asked, bending down to see. "Oh my God!" she shrieked. "You're bleeding!"

The popsicle, and my attempts to pry it free, had ripped patches of skin from my face. So now I was sitting there with a frozen dessert fused to my head *and* blood beginning to drip down my shirt.

The White House doctor and nurse were summoned—they were, lucky for me, on the flight—and went to work trying to pop off the popsicle. In the meantime, the rest of the gang, the press pool, the new staff—the president-elect included—were all laughing so hard they nearly wet their collective pants as Dr. Jeff Kuhlman and nurse Shelly Carr started a timely tradition of stitching, stapling, and saving me from myself.

"Reggie," Obama asked incredulously, "what the hell are you doing?"

"I didn't even want the thing!" I sputtered to Obama, while glaring at Marvin.

Obama just looked at me like, "Who eats a popsicle in the middle of winter?"

In the end, it took twenty minutes to remove the popsicle. The doctor tried hot water, glycerin, a whole slew of tactics. I thought they were going to try to pee on it. When it finally loosened its death grip on my skin, I looked like I'd seen the rough end of twelve rounds.

It should be noted that no one else ate a popsicle. And since then, neither have I. Not that it matters. Till this day I still haven't been able to live that moment down.

The old me would have been fatally embarrassed. Sure, it was mortifying—no doubt. But I came to see that being laughed at in the trenches is a part of the process. My humiliations made for good stories. So did everyone else's. Those human moments reminded us that we weren't just machines doing a job, that we were real people behind the professional façade.

Those moments broke down the walls. Not to mention brought down the house.

25

A BUSINESS, MAN

*The first year I worked in the White House, I was totally lost. I only un-*derstood a fraction of what was being talked about in the rooms where I stood. I was always on my BlackBerry, looking stuff up, trying to educate myself. What was H1N1? Why were the Somali pirates so effective? Who was Lech Walesa?

It would have been simpler to just tune out, but I was curious. And it was oddly helpful to know what I didn't know. I figured out that just when I wanted to stop listening was exactly the time when I shouldn't. I was turning myself into a human search engine.

Another part of my job was managing expectations. I had to give the impression that I was poised and in control, even though there were times when I was neither. So when the team ran late, or notes went missing, or appointments were overbooked, I was first on the line of defense, managing not just POTUS's expectations, but the expectations of everyone who wanted to intersect with him.

Ironically, often the best way to do this was to admit I didn't have all the answers. If I said, "That's a good question. I don't know the answer yet," I could diffuse the situation. It put me in the same boat as the person with the anxiety. It was leveling. And admitting what I didn't know (but intended to find out) was much more effective than strutting around and throwing my ego and position in another person's face. I learned that joining people was better than beating them every time.

Holidays and special occasions were my worst nightmare. The asks and expectations became a flood. The administration has to acknowledge everything, with the President as either the host or the guest of honor. Every year, he attends something like thirty Christmas parties, Seders, and countless balls and dinners.

My whole stint at the Oval, I got nervous at every event. I couldn't help myself. It brought me back to my time at Duke, when Coach K drilled into us that each player represented the school, and each of us consequently had a target on our back for those that wanted to see Duke and the team stumble. It takes an average of six weeks to prepare for a state dinner, and for the first, we wanted it to be executed flawlessly. Sadly, this was not the case.

When POTUS took office, his first state dinner was for the Prime Minister of India, Manmohan Singh. As is well documented, Bravo TV reality vultures and fame-seekers Michaele and Tareq Salahi crashed the event, which led to a lot of bad press. The pair passed through security checkpoints and were able to enter the White House to meet the President and Prime Minister Singh as uninvited guests. The breach led to massive security investigations and legal inquiries for all parties, as well as a lot of heated questioning in the social office about how this could have happened. Even though the Salahis were harmless narcissists looking for their fifteen minutes of notoriety, the breach of protocol and security was viewed as threatening—and also as a PR black eye for the new administration.

For their part, the Salahis maintained on national television that they had in fact been invited and were not "crashers." They went so far as to threaten to sue. Their continued press coverage prolonged the headaches. Even the newspapers in India weighed in and wagged their fingers at our perceived incompetence. Finally, after weeks of microscopic scrutiny and intense examination, White House principal deputy counsel Daniel J. Meltzer stated in a letter to the House of Representatives Committee on Homeland Security on December 23, 2009, "We have found no evidence the Salahis were included on any White House access list or guest list. The Salahis were not on the lists for the State Dinner, the Arrival Ceremony, or any other event scheduled for November 24. Indeed there is no record of the Salahis in the White House visitor access system since the beginning of the Obama Administration. Moreover, we have found no evidence that the Salahis called the White House and asked about the proper dress code for the State Dinner."

Needless to say, security was vise-tight from then on out.

Because of Obama's unique persona, and his relatively young age, celebrity intersected at an unprecedented level with his candidacy and election. He was viewed as "cool." Stars wanted to be adjacent to that coolness. One night in Vegas we ordered chips and beers for a card game in the room to celebrate Marvin's birthday. The candidate was exhausted but trying to rally, when his phone rang. It was Charles Barkley saying, "Hey man, I'm in town for Bill Russell's fantasy camp. Let's hang out!" Obama turned to the group of us and said, "Let's just take tomorrow off and go to the Cheetah Club."

He was, of course, joking. I said, "I'm taking a rain check on that the minute you are *ex-President*."

But that's how it went with Obama: people were drawn to him. On the campaign, I met more famous people than I even knew existed. Some were genuine supporters; others just wanted the association. Hip-hop royalty Jay Z and Beyoncé fell decidedly into the first category. They were on Team Obama from the start, and I remember the day the pair met the future president for the first time.

The day was September 27, 2007, also known as "the most exhilarating time of my non-sporting life." The scene was a corner table at the thirty-fifth-floor lobby restaurant of New York City's swanky Mandarin Oriental Hotel. In attendance were Obama, Jay Z, Beyoncé Knowles, and me. I'd grown up experiencing the world through Jay's songs and stories. When the senator realized I was one of the few people on staff who actually knew a lot about Jay Z, he said, "Just give me the seven best songs," profoundly ignorant of the scale of the task he had just given me. Only seven? I ended up selecting:

"Can't Knock the Hustle"—*Reasonable Doubt*
"Some People Hate"—*Blueprint 2*
"Renegade"—*The Blueprint*
"Breathe Easy (Lyrical Exercise)"—*The Blueprint*
"My 1st Song"—*The Black Album*
"Girls, Girls, Girls, pt. 2"—*The Blueprint*
"Crazy in Love"—*Dangerously in Love* (Beyoncé featuring Jay Z)

Obama gave them a thorough listening his next day at the gym, and the playlist went over well enough that he asked for more and, later, for a different artist, for Lil Wayne. (He always gave me credit for the introduction to Jay's music, often telling the press his bodyman turned him on to Hova.)

When we met up in the Mandarin Oriental, Beyoncé was just coming off tour. Obama was discussing how much dancing she did at her concerts, having taken his daughters to a show in Chicago. Beyoncé admitted her feet were killing her.

Obama joked, "You have to have a masseuse to massage your feet. That must be in the budget for the tour production."

And Jay said, "Yeah, so long as it isn't a man."

I quipped, "You've seen *Pulp Fiction*. You never let another man massage your woman's feet," after which Jay burst out laughing.

★ ★ ★

After that meeting, Jay Z was actively involved in the campaign, helping to send voters to polling stations, performing for free at voter-drive concerts, and generally spreading the word and communicating the value of Obama's election to his millions of fans.

The senator saw Jay as a good guy, smart and hardworking, who he believed would "help shape attitudes in a real positive way." Which is exactly what came to pass in May 2012, when Jay announced his approval of the President's support of marriage equality.

Just as I clued Obama in to facets of youth culture, he did the same for me with cultural history. I remember I was with the senator when Paul Newman passed away. He read the news in the paper and said what a shame it was.

My response: "The salad dressing guy?"

The candidate looked at me with something like pity and said, "*Cool Hand Luke? Butch Cassidy and the Sundance Kid? Hud? Cat on a Hot Tin Roof?* Anything?"

I needed to do my due diligence, a checklist that extended well past Mr. Newman. Our conversations often became mini-research assignments I gave myself: listen to Elvis Costello; watch *M*A*S*H*; read about JFK, Jimmy Carter. It was a productive exchange. I taught Obama about cloud computing, Dropbox, and his iPad. (The first few times he used it he thought it was broken; I had to explain that the device was in airplane mode.) He enlightened me about Burma, the Ohio Players, and Mormonism.

Our dynamic was a microcosm of what was happening in my larger life. Now that I was out of North Carolina and not playing on a sports team, I spent all day, every day, with people I would never have hung out with otherwise. The changeover taught me that black, white, male, female, Ivy League, community college, young, old, Republican, Democrat, line cook, President—fundamentally, we're all the same and we all have something to teach each other, even if it's only that we have more in common than we're often willing to acknowledge. We all sometimes find ourselves in crap relationships. We all have issues with our parents. We all regret our haircuts in high school.

It sounds basic, but when you surround yourself only with people who share your background and interests, you miss out on feeling a part of the larger social fabric. And that ends up limiting you.

If I'd only ever identified myself as a basketball player and selected a social circle that reflected exclusively that same message, I would have not only been wrong, I would have missed out on the adventure of several lifetimes. I *am* an athlete. But I am *also* a stellar organizer, a public speaker, an environmentalist, a world traveler, a decent cook, a systems analyst, a businessman, and in a few years I hope, a business, man. Putting myself in unfamiliar circles, and necessarily exposing myself to criticism and laughs, showed me time and again that there was more to me than even I knew.

This realization came into full bloom on my twenty-seventh birthday, for which I threw a party in a local dive bar. I wanted to invite all my closest friends, past and present, to come to D.C. The election six months earlier still carried allure with my friends, and many of them desperately wanted a chance to be a part of history being made, by working in a visit to the White House, maybe take pictures in the Oval.

So I invited grade school buddies, old teammates, family members, college roommates, everyone I had ever worked with on the campaign. Problem was, those guests told other people, and by eight-forty-five the party had swelled from twenty attendees to almost a thousand people. It was a legitimate blowout. Duhon bartended. We all danced to my iPod. The shindig made the *Washington Post*.

More vitally to me, the party allowed me to show my appreciation for all the individuals who had helped shape me into the man I was becoming. The President did the same on his own birthdays.

On his forty-ninth, we organized the now legendary basketball games with four teams including LeBron James, Alonzo Mourning, Shane Battier, Chris Paul, Derrick Rose, and Maya Moore. For his gift, he wanted a highly competitive game. He got one. Obama's team lost.

The parties were celebrations in every sense. A way to honor where we'd been, and a light to illuminate where we were going. Both Obama and I wanted to do something nice for the people we loved; to remind ourselves where we'd come from, and how short this journey called life actually is, and to acknowledge—and pay back— the debts we accumulate along the way.

26

75 PERCENT OF LIFE IS JUST SHOWING UP

*When I was young, I thought I wanted to be a radiologist. I did an intern-*ship in high school at Carolinas Medical Center, with Dr. Denise Cassani. I sat in a dark room with Dr. Cassani all day, taking notes while reviewing mammograms, X-rays, and CT scans. I enjoyed the specificity of the job. And the idea of being able to help people. Radiology was also a bit like looking at the map of a patient's future, and that appealed to me. Seeing the array of images produced felt like a scientific tea leaf–reading exercise, granting me (and much more importantly the doctors) a glimpse into what direction patients were headed in life.

It was a question I'd long held about my own prospects, especially after the realization that I couldn't count on a lifelong professional sports career. But I wasn't sure what the best alternative path was for me. Then I met the junior United States senator from the state of Illinois and threw myself down the unfamiliar road less traveled.

Anyone who works out consistently understands muscle memory. When you train long enough, your body internalizes the responses it knows you want it to have; your body and mind are no longer thinking, but just simply reacting seamlessly and effortlessly.

Obama possessed keen muscle memory, his most dominant muscle being his brain. On the campaign especially, there were countless times when his physical body was completely fatigued and as drained as that of a prizefighter who had gone the distance. And yet he would still be able to speak eloquently about complex issues and answer questions about any topic thrown at him. He'd recall names and numbers. He'd have each fact straight and every study memorized. Everyone knows the man is brilliant. But few people have seen up close just exactly how well he is able to perform under demanding circumstances. He'd trained. So he could show up.

I remember when we lost the Nevada caucus in January 2008. Shortly after that was the MLK holiday, and Obama was scheduled to give an early morning speech at Ebenezer Baptist Church, where MLK's family members were appearing. We were staying at the Atlanta Hyatt Regency. The candidate had gotten a copy of the speech the night before. But it wasn't what he wanted. "Too much Old Testament, not enough New Testament," he said.

So he started writing. I typed the edits into the computer. Emailed the draft back and forth to the speechwriters. He was up until almost four o'clock doing oration triage.

At daybreak, I went to wake the candidate for the 8 A.M. service. The campaign rule was, don't enter his room without his permission, a sign of respect for him and the process, but also a formal boundary that no one ever broke. The rule of thumb was to knock and let the senator answer the door. But the Hyatt had given him a massive suite, and I fretted that maybe he couldn't hear me knocking and ringing the doorbell or, even worse, that he was still asleep. I pounded on the door. I waited. I knocked again. Several minutes passed. It was at the point where we were going to be late for church. I asked the agent posted at the door of his room to let me in.

I fumbled blind into the entryway. The room was pitch-black.

"Sir, sir," I said. "It's seven. We need to go."

I groped around, unable to see anything. Then from the darkness I heard him let loose a string of expletives.

He didn't sound angry so much as tired, dead tired. How could any normal person not be? It is one thing to pull an all-nighter to write a paper, but it's another thing when the writer has to read the paper in public less than five hours after writing it on less than four hours' sleep.

"Sir, are you okay?"

"I am just exhausted," he sighed.

The candidate had been dealing with four primaries in a month. He'd only been home one day since Christmas.

I yelled the least welcome news into the darkness: "Sir, you need to be dressed in half an hour."

The senator found his suit, threw it on, and prepared himself in ten quick minutes. The muscle memory kicked in. By the time we reached the church, he was animated and enthusiastic, his brain well and truly primed. At the pulpit, with Coretta Scott King and the rest of the King family front and center in the audience, he delivered one of the most rousing speeches before or since. He said, in part:

What Dr. King understood is that if just one person chose to walk instead of ride the bus, those walls of oppression would not be moved. But maybe if a few more walked, the foundation might start to shake. If a few more women were willing to do what Rosa Parks had done, maybe the cracks would start to show. If teenagers took freedom rides from North to South, maybe a few bricks would come loose. Maybe if white folks marched because they had come to understand that their freedom too was at stake in the impending battle, the wall would begin to sway. And if enough Americans were awakened to the injustice; if they joined together, North and South, rich and poor, Christian and Jew, then perhaps that wall would come tumbling down, and justice would flow like water, and righteousness like a mighty stream.

Unity is the great need of the hour—the great need of this hour. Not because it sounds pleasant or because it makes us feel good, but because it's the only way we can overcome the essential deficit that exists in this country. I'm not talking about a budget deficit. I'm not talking about a trade deficit. I'm not talking about a deficit of good ideas or new plans. I'm talking about a moral deficit. I'm talking about an empathy deficit. I'm talking about an inability to recognize ourselves in one another; to understand that we are our brother's keeper; we are our sister's keeper; that, in the words of Dr. King, we are all tied together in a single garment of destiny.

The Scripture tells us that we are judged not just by word, but by the deed. And if we are to truly bring about the unity that is so crucial in this time, we must find it within ourselves to act on what we know; to understand that living up to this country's ideals and its possibilities will require great effort and resources; sacrifice and stamina.

That morning at Ebenezer, the candidate was calling on all of us to not passively wait for change, but to become instigators. He told us that "each of us carries with us the task for changing our hearts and minds." Like Dr. King, he knew it would take vigor and persistence and the force of the many to make change. To keep America great, we *all* needed to show up.

I saved the paper with his handwritten notes. Later I returned it to him because I knew the speech would be a part of his history, and I thought the paper would remind him how deep you have to dig inside of yourself in order to pull off that winning play we all dream of. Touched, he said if we were lucky it would find a home in the future Presidential Library. The speech is a piece of history now. A piece I held in my hands and had a small part in making happen.

27

KNOW WHEN TO LEAVE THE PARTY

In the summer of 2010, I started volunteering as a mentor at Capital Partners for Education, CPFE, an organization that guides low-income D.C.-area kids toward better circumstances via partnerships with schools, tuition assistance, and skills development. The program is a huge success. Almost 100 percent of the mentees end up attending college.

I played basketball with Khari Brown, the executive director of CPFE, and he told me there was a shortage of male mentors, specifically African-American. Then he asked how I'd feel about becoming one.

I thought about the offer for a minute, then decided, why not? I had benefited from mentors throughout my life, and giving back made simple sense. I learned quickly, though, that I had no idea what

I was getting myself into. I went through the training, which was thorough. We had to know how to handle any situation that might arise. If the kid you're mentoring does X, you do Y. I soon realized it was serious business. I also gained greater respect for the mentors I had encountered who had done their jobs so well.

I met my mentee, Cal, when he was fourteen years old. His father had been incarcerated. His mother lived down the block from him, but was largely absent. Cal was being raised by his grandmother, Shirley. The first thing we did together was go to lunch at Hops, a chain restaurant. When I was Cal's age, going to a place like Hops—he ordered what he always orders, fried chicken—felt like winning the food lottery. I also chose it because it was close to his grandmother's Arlington, Virginia, home and the rec center where Cal spent most of his time. While we ate, I told him who I was and what I did for a living. I shared my basketball history, and I could tell he was pleased to hear my record, particularly me playing at Duke. He was assessing me as much as I was assessing him, and I'm pretty sure I could see his relief once he figured out that we could relate. I'd played college sports. He dreamed of playing college sports. I asked him if he had a girlfriend, and his grin and laugh insinuated that he considered himself to be quite the ladies' man. Just like that, we'd found common ground.

Since that lunch, we see each other every couple weeks. We hang out, eat, shoot hoops. Mostly we do schoolwork together. When we're apart, we email and text. I give him my advice, which he doesn't ask for. Cal wants to play college ball. And he just might. But I try to stress the value of education above all.

"The reason I've had access to opportunities is because of my education," I explain to him as often as I can. "Don't be afraid to ask questions. No one has all the answers."

I tell him the things that I heard as a young man that stuck with me. Eat your vegetables. Condoms are cheaper than diapers. Stand up straight. Make eye contact. Speak clearly. Don't lie. They're all clichés until you actually try to live by them. I think Cal believes he has things under control. He doesn't. I was the same way. Teenage boys are conditioned to not show any vulnerability. To fake it till they make it. Seeing the big picture and letting it inform responsibility isn't their strong suit. Learning that can require some blunt advice delivered repeatedly, something my dad excelled at and I benefited from, albeit sometimes belatedly. I, too, was lost and confused when I was Cal's age. I can see that now. I can also now see that some of my parents' least welcome advice—like pushing me into Providence Day—was the best advice.

I know Cal isn't exactly embracing all the pearls of wisdom I try to impart. But maybe, in time, the words I say to him will sink in, and he will have the strength of them in his back pocket when I'm not around anymore to remind him of what ends up being important in life. Any pearl of advice is only as good as what you eventually do with it.

During high school, Cal transferred from a more rigorous academic program to a less prestigious school so he could get more playing time on the basketball team. It broke my heart a bit, but I understood. He derives his self-worth from what he can do on the court. I can certainly relate. But I hope to show him he is more than a baller. Just as someone showed me.

When I first met Obama, I'd barely journeyed outside of North Carolina. Since we began working together, I've seen sixty-five countries. I've visited every state. I've traveled 1.8 million miles, give or take. My mom jokes that I've "lived five lifetimes" already. I thought Duke was going to be the best education I could have, and it was indeed fortifying, but it can't compare to traveling the world as personal aide to President Obama.

I was twenty-three years old when I moved to D.C. to join the Obama team, and thirty years old when I left. I grew up in his company. Became a man. And, just as is the case with every young person who comes of age, once I realized I'd matured, I slowly started to figure out that it was time to move on.

When I committed to follow the President into the West Wing, I promised two years. I ended up staying three. Even then, the choice to exit was fraught for me. I had so much respect for the President and what he was doing, and continues to do, for our country.

I backed into the discussion instead. I'd been attending business school while I was working as his White House PA, taking classes on the weekends and studying late at night and early in the mornings. I'd bitten off more than I could chew and my grades reflected that. Knowing how much Obama valued education, I brought up my dilemma with him.

"I wanted to get your thoughts," I asked one afternoon.

"Sure thing, Reg."

"School is kind of kicking my ass," I said. "I'm not doing well, I'm potentially going to get kicked out because of my performance. I don't know what you think, but I wanted to know whether or not you believed it made more sense for me to spend more time focusing on school."

It was, I acknowledge, a bit of a passive-aggressive approach. But I was conflicted. And I didn't ever want to let the team down, especially him.

"Well, you made it this far, you might as well finish it out and see it through," the President answered. I exhaled a sigh of relief.

This was a progression in his philosophy. When I'd initially asked him a few months earlier about graduate school, he was ambivalent. I needed him to sign off on my missing work every other Friday and Saturday for classes, and he wasn't crazy about that plan. He thought it would be unfair to the other staffers who didn't get those days off. He also sensed that being both a personal aide and a grad student would be more than I could handle.

"I need to go to grad school because I don't want people to say ten years from now that the only reason I am where I am is because I worked for Barack Obama," I blurted.

"You're never going to get away from that," the President said.

"Yeah, I know, but I need to have other credentials for people to take me seriously."

Obama felt he had given me the best advice he could. While no one valued education more than the President, no one was more committed to taking full responsibility for the opportunity his office presented to improve the lives of the greatest number of Americans as possible. But the very fact that I was being stubborn about this is what made our relationship so unique. Leaving that job is hard for anyone who has ever had it. But I trusted my instincts. Two habits, incidentally, I had learned from the best.

Once he knew there would be no swaying me, the President became a huge supporter of my new goal. He let me leave a month early.

Playing sports hones your powers of observation. You become adept at seeing the big picture and visualizing where you fit into it. For years, I'd figured out where I fit on the team and maximized my position within that framework. But my personal season was ending. I wanted school to help prepare me for my next step. It was my time to leave.

The day I packed up my desk, I recalled something else Bush's former PA Jared had told me when I started. He said, "This journey is like no other. But know that it all comes to an end."

I was lucky. My job ended. But my relationships did not. Saying goodbye turned out to not be goodbye at all. Obama and I still see each other. Sometimes we play cards, shoot hoops, or swing clubs. Sometimes we still correspond about the same things we used to talk about in person. Nothing serious or work-related. We talk basketball. We talk life. We talk like friends.

28

CREATE YOUR OWN SHOT

I still play basketball every morning I can. Old habits die hard. Some-
times I play with the President, but most of the time I play with my
friends. I mentor kids now, and I recently went to my sixteen-year-
old mentee's AAU basketball game in Paterson, New Jersey. There I
was, sitting on a hard seat in a high school gym, eating hot dogs and
cheering him on. It was the happiest I'd been in a long time.

I guess when it comes right down to it, I'm a simple guy. I know
how it feels to live small and large, and in truth, the things that give
me satisfaction don't change. Sweet tea. People who smile and say,
"Good morning." The stirring swell of a church choir. The Bojangles'
dark-meat box. A pickup game at dusk in the park. Playing spades
with the family. Beer pong night with buddies. My mother saying
she's proud of me. My father shooting hoops with me.

Some of my best memories are of driving around small towns in the South with my dad. Before there was an Air Force One. Or celebrities. Or heads of state. Or Secret Service. When there was just me playing in a ratty gym, eating at Golden Corral.

A day doesn't go by in which I don't think about how lucky I am to be called a Love. Life can be cruel. There are tons of people who have worked harder than me and have a fraction of what I have to show for it. That's not because they aren't smart or talented. It's just the hand we're dealt.

★ ★ ★

Dreams come and go. What feels like the end is often just the beginning. If you are in a valley, you have to know you aren't going to stay down forever. And when you are riding high, that won't last either. Everything levels out in the end, and if you keep that in mind, you can manage your feelings through the best and worst of times.

I learned that first from my father, who gave me my start and my spine. The best dad a kid could ask for, he was present and proud—of me, of our family, of the position we carved out in our community. He, with my mother, equipped me with the tools for success and made sure I knew how to use them. Of all the men I have ever met, he is the man I most hope I can become.

Coach K conditioned me and taught me how to be on a team and accountable to the team, as he has done for countless other young men under his tutelage. He steered me away from my ego and my indignation, from my self-destructive asshattery and toward a bigger picture that wasn't all about me. He prepared me for the real world in ways I didn't come to understand until many years later. The work I did on his teams ended up being less about three-pointers and rebounds and more about discovering my character, integrity, and how good it could feel to sacrifice. In short, he turned me into an adult.

Without that growth, I would never have met President Barack Obama, who showed me not only a blueprint for tackling problems head-on, but what is possible for a man like me in this country. He has often said his story could only happen in America, and I believe him to be correct.

Unlike that single-minded kid from North Carolina who only cared about winning basketball games, I am no longer oblivious to the world's concerns. Nor am I naïve. But I do believe. Like my former boss, I have the audacity of hope.

All three of these men have instilled in me the unshakable faith that our potential is limitless.

And I know, sure as I know there is no music as beautiful as the swish of a net, that there is nothing we can't achieve, if we just stand tall, take the ball, and power forward.

ACKNOWLEDGING OTHERS

One of the most important lessons I have learned is to express thanks to the people and teammates who have helped you and your team achieve success. I remember sitting in the locker room at Duke watching tape as a player for Coach K; he would often highlight when a connecting play was made—when a screen was set to create an open shot or when a comrade drew a charge. I often saw Barack Obama do the same thing at town halls and rallies when he would thank the people behind the scenes. Both he and Coach K knew that no one can shoulder the entire load. And I would be foolish to believe that my experiences are the result of my actions alone.

My family is the best support group any person could ever have. When I was growing up, Edward and Netta Vanderhorst loved me like they were my parents, and their sons Kiawah, Jervay, and Ade were brothers to me. My cousins Jasmine, Jessica, Jennifer, and Valerie were the sisters I never had but always wanted. My cousins Lynn, Matt, and James always pushed me to keep up with them. Frankie Poole, my workout partner and motivator over the holidays, never missed a day in pushing me to get better, even on Thanksgiving and

Christmas. Gloretha Mercer, Raymond Jackson, Maureen and Tim Price, my surrogate parents, the aunts and uncle who supported me every step of the way. Alice Poole, Wesley Jackson, Jimmy Mercer, and Ann Hitchcock—in their loving memory, I know they are still with me today.

The Providence Day School community took me in with open arms and nourished my academic career at a very critical junction. I appreciate the teachers and administrators who not only pushed me but also held me accountable: Rhea Caldwell, Kay Montross, Eric Hedinger, Ted Dickson, John Patterson, David Carrier, Joe Fortier, Jim Cerbie, and Grant Coffey; and my teammates and classmates: David Callaway, Erik Stowe, Mike Dames, Derek Fricke, Brett Golembe, Brendan Rowell, Trent Cherry, Marcus Oliver, Jake Blau, Ryan Carson, Keith Fehring, and many others. The leadership of individuals like Glyn Cowlishaw, Ben Robinson, and Robert Toth has not only had an impact on me but has shown me the importance of continued investment in our youth and our community.

Duke University is a school that I'm immensely proud to have attended. The friendships forged during the victories and defeats are ones that I will never forget, including teammates like Nate Krill, Jeremy Battier, BJ Hill, Charles Porter, Ryan Fowler, Daryl Scott, Khary Sharpe, Chris Duhon, Kyle Moore, Josh Krieder, Luke Bayer, Troy Austin, Ben Erdeljac, Cory Broadnax, Dee Bryant, Adam Smith, Spencer Romine, Bobby Campbell, Chris Dapolito, Mike Schneider, Daniel Ewing, J. J. Redick, Sheldon Williams, Lee Melchionni, Sean Dockery, Shav Randolph, Dave McClure, Mike Dunleavy, Jason Williams, Andre Buckner, Matt Christianson, Andy Borman, Andy Means, Ryan Caldbeck, Casey Sanders, Terrell Smith, Joe Pagliuca, Patrick Johnson, and every Blue Team Bomber past and present.

The staff from the football and basketball programs often felt like family. Every word of encouragement and every piece of constructive criticism were part of my growth from an eighteen-year-old kid to a collegiate athlete and a college graduate. Without people like Chris Collins, Aubrey Hill, Steve Wojciechowski, Johnny Dawkins, David Cuttcliffe, Fred Chatham, Scottie Montgomery, and Joe DeLamielleure, I would have missed out on the most important opportunities for personal and athletic growth. And I could never forget Ms. Gerry Brown, Ms. Laura Ann Howard, Ms. Micky Laws, and Ms. Peggy Nelson. Their warm smiles and inspiring levels of energy always made a trip to the coaching offices a little homier; they were like surrogate mothers for me the first time I was really away from my own mother. And though not a coach, Malbert and the MetaMetrics family nourished my inquisitive side.

My first journey outside of sports was the summer I spent two months in Indianapolis, where the closest I got to organized sports was running into Chris Paul while he was still in high school and competing at Nike Camp at NIFS. I couldn't have had a better group to welcome me to a job and a city that were foreign to me than Alan and Joann Hogan, Susan and David Rimstidt and their family, John and Karen Fernandez, Angie Gates, Lori Lambert, Adairius Gardner, Kyle Willis, Betty Cochran, and Pat and Sharon Robbins. Because of your support and openness, to this day I still feel like I'm half Hoosier.

Hello, Washington, D.C. While I walked through the halls of the Hart Senate building at twenty-three years of age in my brown, square-toed Kenneth Coles and my nondescript beige tie, my friends and colleagues never ridiculed me or looked at me sideways because of my antiquated attire, at least not that I could tell. Thanks to Kristen Jarvis, Ashley Tate-Gilmore, Michael Strautmanis, Robert Gibbs, Jon Favreau, Tommy Vietor, Alyssa Mastromonaco, Pete Rouse, LaDarius Curtis, Karen Richardson, Emily Bokar, Mark Lippert, Danny Sepulveda, Nick Bauer, Josh DuBois, Jim Brayton, Carolyn Mosely, Jordan Kaplan, Jenny Yeager, and Tori Scarborough.

The endless days and sleepless nights of working on the campaign and in the White House would have been far less manageable and enjoyable without the RONs: Ellie Sue Schafer, Cookie Offerman, and Dana Lewis; the Iowa state team led by Paul Tewes and Emily Parcel; the scheduling advance team of Jessica Wright, Danielle Crutchfield, Emmett Beliveau, Chase Cushman, Ferial Govashiri, Brian Mosteller, Katie Johnson, Anita Decker, Greg Lorjuste, Mike Brush, Dave Cusack, Tim Hartz, Duncan Teater, and Kenny Thompson.

To the D.C. hoops crew: who would have known there are people willing to play basketball at six in the morning without the chance of ever making a penny? True love for the game is hard to find, and when you do it is something unbelievably special. Thank you to Art Jackson, John Rice, Arne Duncan, and all of the guys in the run for letting me crash the game.

And to my D.C. crew: thanks for keeping me grounded and not giving me too much shit when I always underestimated my arrival times—Erik Stowe, Brooks Brown, Kat Conlon, John McNaught, Shomik Dutta, Peter Friedlander, James Evans, Carissa Aiello, Julius Genachowski, and my brother, Richard Love Jr.

To the Campathlon crew: you all are the true definition of friendship. The President is lucky to have such a loyal group of friends. I have learned so much about friendship and loyalty from you all: Marvin Nicholson, Sam Kass, Cornell McClelan, Marty Nesbitt, Eric Whitaker, Greg Orme, Michal Ramos, Bobby Titcomb, Hassan Chandoo, Wahid Hamid, and Laurent Delanney.

To Lorenzo Roccia, Abel Navarro, Danilo Diazganado, Carlos Hajj, Guillermo Fernandez, Aaron Dowd, and the entire Transatlantic team: thanks for taking a chance on me. A great journey to date that I'm sure will only continue to get better.

To the entire Chicago crew: Mayor Rahm Emanuel, Mike Faulman, Mike Ruemmler, and all of the team that continues to make Chicago one of the greatest cities; Jon Carson, Kathy Gasperine, Jim Messina, and the entire OFA team that continues to push for change from the bottom up; thanks to John Rogers, the Crown family, the Pritzker family, Les and Javon Coney, the Heymans, Bob Clark, Jim Reynolds, Richard Price, Parham, and the McKeevers.

To Orin Kramer, Brian Mathis, Robert Wolf, Mark Gallogly, and Richard Plepler: New York is a crazy place, and I thank you for helping me learn how to navigate it.

To Mark Emmert and my good friend Commissioner Adam Silver—thank you for nourishing and growing the game of basketball, which has not only taught me valuable life lessons but has given me so many great opportunities and a lifetime of friendships.

To every person who worked on this book and helped make it possible: Jonathan Karp, Thomas LeBien, Julia Prosser, Jofie Ferrari-Adler, Julianna Haubner, Anna Ruch, Bob Barnett, Deneen Howell, Helen Syski, David Fisher, and the entire teams at Simon & Schuster and Williams & Connolly. And a special thanks to Allison Glock.

To all of the NFC members and field organizers on the 2008 and 2012 campaigns: thank you for everything that you have done and all of your hard work. And to anyone whom I may have left off: I truly appreciate you all.

Lastly but most importantly: to my father and mother, Richard and Lynette Love, and the President and First Lady, Barack and Michelle Obama—thank you for always continuing to invest in me.

ABOUT THE AUTHOR

Reggie Love was the special assistant and personal aide to President Barack Obama from 2007 to 2011. Before that, he graduated from Duke University, where he was captain of the 2004–05 Duke Blue Devils basketball team and a member of the 2001 NCAA national championship team. Love graduated from the Wharton School of Business in 2013 and now serves as partner and vice president of RON Transatlantic Advisors.